BE STRONG
AND OF GOOD
COURAGE

BE STRONG AND OF GOOD COURAGE

JACK R. CHRISTIANSON

Bookcraft
Salt Lake City, Utah

Library of Congress Catalog Card Number: 94-79642
ISBN 0-88494-957-5

First Printing, 1994

Printed in the United States of America

To Tom, Bonnie, Diann, and Becky—
for helping me dream dreams and for
forever showing their love.

"There shall not any man be able to stand before thee all the days of thy life: as I was with Moses, so I will be with thee: I will not . . . forsake thee.

Be strong and of a good courage. . . .

Have not I commanded thee? Be strong and of a good courage; be not afraid, neither be thou dismayed: for the Lord thy God is with thee whithersoever thou goest."

—*Joshua 1:5–6, 9*

Contents

Acknowledgments

As always, a book such as this could never have been published without the help of many. A special appreciation to my beloved Melanie, who continually supports me and types my difficult-to-read manuscripts. Thanks also to Stan Johnson for his help in obtaining treasured quotes from the prophets and Apostles; to Deseret Book for permission to include the chapter "Withstanding Sexual Pressure," an earlier version of which appeared in their book *Why Say No When the World Says Yes;* to Cory Maxwell for his interest in my writing and his editorial skills; and to the kind and talented staff at Bookcraft, who give such insightful suggestions.

A special appreciation for the strength, courage, and example of my dear friends Jeff Geertsen and Taylor Manning.

1

Dreaming Dreams and Seeing Visions

On the evening of September 21, 1823, an incredible event transpired that forever changed the history of this earth. In his own words, an inquiring seventeen-year-old boy, Joseph Smith, Jr., knelt in "prayer and supplication to Almighty God for forgiveness of all my sins and follies, and also for a manifestation to me, that I might know of my state and standing before him" (JS-H 1:29).

Like so many of us, Joseph sought forgiveness and a knowledge of how he fared with his Maker. He "had full confidence in obtaining a divine manifestation, as [he] previously had one" (JS-H 1:29). The result of this prayer of faith was the appearance of an angelic minister named Moroni. Joseph described Moroni and then said that when he first looked at the heavenly messenger, Joseph was afraid, but the fear soon left him (see JS-H 1:30–32).

As we ponder this account, we must ask the question,

What was so significant about Moroni's message that it took the entire night and part of the next day to deliver? Joseph said that the angel appeared three times during the night and then again the following morning as Joseph attempted to go home after working with his father. Each time Moroni repeated "the very same things which he had done at his first visit, without the least variation" (JS-H 1:45). Four visits in less than twenty-four hours, and each visit brought the same angel declaring the same exact message!

What was the message? Of course, Joseph learned about several things, including the gold plates, upon which was written the Book of Mormon, their location, and the existence and use of the Urim and Thummim (see JS-H 1:34–35, 42). But could that have taken the entire night? What else was Joseph told that had such significance? For one, he was told his name would be "had for good and evil among all nations, kindreds, and tongues, or that it should be both good and evil spoken of among all people" (JS-H 1:33).

After these humbling messages were given, something else incredible occurred. Moroni began quoting certain Old Testament prophecies. Imagine, in the midst of this sacred, pristine experience, a messenger from God quoted scriptures from the book so many feel is boring and difficult to understand. I wonder how many of us would have quit listening right there? Why the Old Testament? Why quote scriptures at all? Was Moroni bringing one of the most significant messages that any personage from God's presence could bring—that is, that the Lord keeps his promises and fulfills *all* the words of his holy prophets from the beginning of time?

Moroni quoted the third and fourth chapters of Malachi with a little variation from the King James edition of the Bible. He quoted the eleventh chapter of

Isaiah and said it was about to be fulfilled. He then cited Acts 3:22–23 precisely as those verses stand in our New Testament. With each of these quotations, Moroni gave some explanation. Then he quoted Joel 2:28–32 and said "that this was not yet fulfilled, but was soon to be" (see JS-H 1:36–41). To me, this last is the most interesting quote of the experience. Why? Because, how many of us spend time in the book of Joel? Yet, what Joel prophesied is at the heart of this chapter and the entire book:

> And it shall come to pass afterward, that I will pour out my spirit upon all flesh; and your sons and your daughters shall prophesy, your old men shall dream dreams, your young men shall see visions:
>
> And also upon the servants and upon the handmaids in those days will I pour out my spirit.
>
> And I will shew wonders in the heavens and in the earth, blood, and fire, and pillars of smoke.
>
> The sun shall be turned into darkness, and the moon into blood, before the great and the terrible day of the Lord come.
>
> And it shall come to pass, that whosoever shall call on the name of the Lord shall be delivered: for in mount Zion and in Jerusalem shall be deliverance, as the Lord hath said, and in the remnant whom the Lord shall call. (Joel 2:28–32.)

The Lord will pour out his spirit upon all flesh, and many will prophesy; many will dream dreams, and many will see visions!

Do you dare to dream dreams? Do you have visions of the future? Do you testify of truth? The book of Revelation says that "the testimony of Jesus is the spirit of prophesy" (Revelation 19:10).

I'm not talking about just having a positive mental attitude. I'm talking about your becoming what you truly dream about becoming and about your then helping the Lord to "pour out [his] spirit upon all flesh."

President Spencer W. Kimball had a vision of the future and dreamed dreams of our potential. He stated:

> In our world, there have risen brilliant stars in drama, music, literature, sculpture, painting, science, and all the graces. For long years I have had a vision of members of the Church greatly increasing their already strong positions of excellence till the eyes of all the world will be upon us.
>
> President John Taylor so prophesied, as he emphasized his words with this directive:
>
> "You mark my words, and write them down and see if they do not come to pass.
>
> "You will see the day that Zion will be far ahead of the outside world in everything pertaining to learning of every kind as we are today in regard to religious matters.
>
> "God expects Zion to become the praise and glory of the whole earth, so that kings hearing of her fame will come and gaze upon her glory. . . ." (Sermon, September 20, 1857; see *The Messenger*, July 1953.) . . . Our day, our time, our people, our generation should produce such as we catch the total vision of our potential, dream dreams, and see visions of the future. (*Education for Eternity*, Brigham Young University Speeches of the Year [Provo, 12 September 1967], pp. 12–13.)

We must dare to dream! The Lord needs good, honest, faithful sons and daughters in all areas of expertise. Do you dream of being a great actor or actress? Then be one. Do you want to be a great teacher, doctor, lawyer, homemaker, scientist, engineer, truck driver, farmer, salesperson? Then be the best you can be! If you want to write, then write!

But, as we pursue our dreams and see our visions realized, we must always remember to keep the Lord in his proper place in our lives, and then all other priorities will stay in their proper places. As we keep the Lord at the focal point, hopefully we will not put professional dreams and visions ahead of serving missions, marrying in the temple, and making and keeping sacred covenants. When these important steps in our lives are fulfilled, the Lord can better "pour out [his] spirit upon all flesh." When the Lord is number one in our lives, we will not forget why we must dream our dreams and see our visions of the future. We must do so in hopes that all people—of all races, colors, creeds, and religions—can have the Spirit poured out upon them and come to know our Father, the only true God, and Jesus Christ, whom he has sent (see John 17:3).

Elder Richard G. Scott has taught: "Now, the most important principle I can share: Anchor your life in Jesus Christ, your Redeemer. Make your Eternal Father and his Beloved Son the most important priority in your life— more important than life itself, more important than a beloved companion or children or anyone on earth. Make their will your central desire. Then all that you need for happiness will come to you." (*Ensign,* May 1993, p. 34.)

It will come to you! You cannot force happiness. At times some people appear to be trying so desperately to find and keep happiness that they are miserable! They seek happiness with drugs, alcohol, and parties while lusting for money, fame, and immoral practices. In the end, however, many find only sorrow, heartbreak, and emptiness. Happiness is a by-product of sincerely following the Father and his Son and of making and keeping sacred covenants. Happiness cannot be forced any more than a plant can be forced to grow. We must do all we can and then wait for the Savior (the tree of life; see 1 Nephi 11:21–24) and our Father to bring forth fruit unto us. Alma said it this way, "Then, my brethren, ye shall reap the rewards of your faith, and your diligence, and patience, and long-suffering, waiting for the tree to bring forth fruit unto you" (Alma 32:43). Then, we must not forget that in the vision of the tree of life, the fruit of the tree was "desirable to make one happy" (1 Nephi 8:10).

It is also impossible to force ourselves to be spiritual. In fact, when we try to force the Spirit, we open ourselves up to be deceived.

We must let happiness, the Spirit, and spiritual gifts come as God grants them to us. When we put our Father and his Son at the center of our lives, these gifts will flow unto us "without compulsory means . . . forever and ever" (see D&C 121:46).

Elder Boyd K. Packer, while speaking at Brigham Young University, taught a valuable lesson concerning the receiving of such spiritual gifts as happiness and the Spirit:

> I must emphasize that the word "gift" is of great significance, for a gift may not be demanded or it ceases to be a gift. It may only be accepted when proffered.
>
> Inasmuch as spiritual gifts are gifts, the conditions under which we may receive them are established by him who offers them to us. Spiritual gifts cannot be forced, for a gift is a gift. They cannot, I repeat, be forced, nor bought, nor "earned" in the sense that we make some gesture in payment and expect them to automatically be delivered on our own terms.
>
> There are those who seek such gifts with such persistence that each act moves them further from them. And in that persistence and determination they place themselves in spiritual danger. Rather we are to live to be worthy of the gifts and they will come according to the will of the Lord. ("Gifts of the Spirit," Brigham Young University Sixteen-Stake Fireside, Provo, Utah: 4 January 1987.)

Then, with the Spirit, we can dream dreams and see visions of the future. Without it, we cannot do all that we could nor can we see things clearly "as they really are, and . . . as they really will be" (Jacob 4:13).

The Apostle Paul taught this principle in his letter to the Galatians. He said, "This I say then, Walk in the Spirit, and ye shall not fulfill the lust of the flesh. For the flesh lusteth against the Spirit, and the Spirit against the flesh: and these are contrary the one to the other: so that ye cannot do the things that ye would." (Galatians 5:16–17.)

Paul further instructed us in what the works of the flesh and the works of the Spirit are. He taught that we should not seek the fruits of the Spirit in order to obtain vain glory. Again, everything we do should build our Father's kingdom and allow his Spirit to be poured out on all flesh:

> But if ye be led of the Spirit, ye are not under the law.
> Now the works of the flesh are manifest, which are these; Adultery, fornication, uncleanness, lasciviousness,
> Idolatry, witchcraft, hatred, variance, emulations, wrath, strife, seditions, heresies,
> Envyings, murders, drunkenness, revellings, and such like: of the which I tell you before, as I have also told you in time past, that they which do such things shall not inherit the kingdom of God.
> But the fruit of the Spirit is love, joy, peace, longsuffering, gentleness, goodness, faith,
> Meekness, temperance: against such there is no law.
> And they that are Christ's have crucified the flesh with the affections and lusts.
> If we live in the Spirit, let us also walk in the Spirit.
> Let us not be desirous of vain glory, provoking one another, envying one another. (Galatians 5:17–26.)

President Kimball's dream and vision of the arts continues with these sobering words:

> For years I have been waiting for someone to do justice in recording in song and story and painting and sculpture the story of the restoration, the re-establishment of the kingdom of God on earth, the struggles and frustrations; the apostasies and inner revolutions and counter revolutions of those first decades; of the exodus; of the counter reactions; of the transitions; of the persecution days; of the plural marriage and the underground; of the miracle man, Joseph Smith, of whom we sing "Oh, what rapture filled his bosom, for he saw the living God!"; and of the giant colonizer and builder, Brigham Young. . . .
>
> The full story of Mormonism has never yet been written nor painted nor sculptured nor spoken. It remains for inspired hearts and talented fingers *yet* to reveal themselves. They must be faithful, inspired, active Church members to give life and feeling and true perspective to a subject so worthy. Such masterpieces should run for months in every movie center, cover every part of the globe in the tongue of the people, written by great artists, purified by the best critics.
>
> Our writers, our motion picture specialists, with the inspiration of heaven, should tomorrow be able to produce a masterpiece which would live forever. Our own talent, obsessed with dynamism from a CAUSE, could put into such a story life and heartbeats and emotions and love and pathos, drama, suffering, fear, courage, and [they could put into it] the great leader, the mighty modern Moses who led a people farther than from Egypt to Jericho, who knew miracles as great as the stream from the rock at Horeb, manna in the desert, giant grapes, rain when needed, battles won against great odds. . . .
>
> Take a Nicodemus and put Joseph Smith's spirit in him and what do you have? Take a da Vinci or a Michelangelo or a Shakespeare and give him a total knowledge of the plan of salvation of God and personal revelation and

cleanse him, and then take a look at the statues he will carve, and the murals he will paint, and the masterpieces he will produce. Take a Handel with his purposeful effort, his superb talent, his earnest desire to properly depict the story, and give him inward vision of the whole true story and revelation and what a master you have!

The architect Daniel H. Burnham said:

> Make no little plans; they have no magic [there]
>   to stir men's blood
> And probably themselves will not be realized.
> Make big plans; aim high and hope and work,
> Remembering that a noble, logical diagram once
>   recorded will never die,
> But long after we are gone,
> Will be a living thing,
> Asserting itself with ever-growing insistency.
> Remember that our sons and grandsons are going
>   to do things
> That would stagger us.
> Let your watchword be order and your beacon
>   beauty.

(*Education for Eternity*, pp. 19–20.)

Somehow, we must catch the vision held by this humble prophet and dare to dream it ourselves.

One problem with dreaming dreams is that we too often fear what others think, say, and do. People will criticize. They will challenge our motives; they will question the sincerity of our hearts. No matter, we must remember the Lord's words as he comforted an unconfident, frightened Moroni writing on the blessed gold plates (remember, this is the same Moroni who, as a resurrected being, appeared to Joseph Smith on 21 September 1823!):

> And I said unto him: Lord, the Gentiles will mock at these things, because of our weakness in writing. . . .

And thou hast made us that we could write but little, because of the awkwardness of our hands. . . .

. . . And I fear lest the Gentiles shall mock at our words.

And when I had said this, the Lord spake unto me, saying: Fools mock, but they shall mourn; and my grace is sufficient for the meek, that they shall take no advantage of your weakness;

And if men come unto me I will show unto them their weakness. I give unto men weakness that they may be humble; and my grace is sufficient for all men that humble themselves before me; for if they humble themselves before me, and have faith in me, then will I make weak things become strong unto them. (Ether 12:23–27.)

Remember, fools mock!

Many stood in the "great and spacious building" pointing the finger of scorn at Lehi and the others who were partaking of the fruit. "But," Lehi tellingly commented, "we heeded them not" (1 Nephi 8:33).

Lehi knew what was important in life. He knew what he needed to do to fulfill his dream of the tree of life; he also saw clearly that "as many as heeded" those in the building "had fallen away" (see 1 Nephi 8:34).

George Bernard Shaw, the Irish dramatist and critic, taught a great lesson when he summed up an approach to life: "Other people see things and say, 'WHY?' But I dream things that never were—and I say, 'WHY NOT?'" President Kimball commented on this statement by declaring, "We need people . . . who can dream of things that never were, and ask 'WHY NOT?'" (*Education for Eternity*, p. 15.)

Has God used up all of his ammunition for the blessing of his children? Are all the great things that need to be done accomplished? Orson F. Whitney thought not. He said, "We shall yet have Miltons and Shakespeares of our own. God's ammunition is not exhausted. His highest spirits are held in reserve for the latter times. In God's name and by his help we will build up a literature whose tops will touch the heaven, though its foundation may now be low on the earth." (As cited in Boyd K. Packer, "The Arts and the Spirit of the Lord," Brigham Young University Twelve-Stake Fireside, 1 February 1976, p. 3.)

President Ezra Taft Benson was one who dared to dream dreams and see visions of the future. His courage in declaring the messages from the Book of Mormon was an example to all of us. His life was proof that he wanted to fulfill Joel's prophecy as given on that memorable evening in 1823. Nearly every time he rose to speak he declared how we as a people must move the Book of Mormon forward in a monumental way (see chapter 7, "Why We Need the Book of Mormon"). For instance, let us read his touching description of his "vision":

> I have a vision of homes alerted, of classes alive, and of pulpits aflame with the spirit of Book of Mormon messages.
>
> I have a vision of home teachers and visiting teachers, ward and branch officers, and stake and mission leaders counseling our people out of the most correct of any book on earth—the Book of Mormon.
>
> I have a vision of artists putting into film, drama, literature, music, and paintings great themes and great characters from the Book of Mormon.
>
> I have a vision of thousands of missionaries going into the mission field with hundreds of passages memorized from the Book of Mormon so that they might feed the needs of a spiritually famished world.
>
> I have a vision of the whole Church getting nearer to God by abiding by the precepts of the Book of Mormon.
>
> Indeed, I have a vision of flooding the earth with the Book of Mormon. (*Ensign,* November 1988, p. 6.)

Hopefully, like President Benson, each of us will "spend all [our] remaining days in that glorious effort" (ibid.). I am confident that we will, if we will ponder what occurred in Joseph's bedroom so long ago. If we can but ask why Moroni quoted what he did from the Old Testament and then have Nephi's courage to desire to "see, and hear, and know of these things, by the power of the Holy Ghost" (1 Nephi 10:17). We will not only dare to dream but also strive to fulfill those dreams. Then, the Spirit will be poured out upon all flesh and the kingdom of God will "become the praise and glory of the whole earth so that kings, hearing of her fame, will come and gaze upon her glory" (John Taylor, *The Gospel Kingdom,* sel. G. Homer Durham [Salt Lake City: Bookcraft, 1964], p. 276).

2

Freedom of Religion

In order to dream dreams and see visions of the future, we must have the freedom to pursue those dreams and fulfill those visions. If we lose our freedom to worship God "according to the dictates of our own conscience" or if we fail to allow "all men the same privilege" (see Articles of Faith 1:11), we have lost the key ingredient to fulfilling the dreams of our hearts and our visions of the future. People must be able to choose for themselves and worship "how, where, or what they may" (ibid.) if the Spirit is to be poured out upon all flesh (see Joel 2:28).

From the very beginning, Satan has sought to destroy the agency of man. He continues to do so today. Without freedom to choose, truth cannot flourish. Lehi taught: "Wherefore, men are free according to the flesh; and all things are given them which are expedient unto man. And they are free to choose liberty and eternal life, through the great Mediator of all men, or to choose captivity and death, according to the captivity and power of the devil; for he seeketh that all men might be miserable like unto himself." (2 Nephi 2:27.) When people are captive, misery follows. Freedom brings not only confidence but also joy and peace.

Freedom of religion as we have today in America and other parts of the world must be preserved at all costs. It is a precious treasure—a treasure that untold millions have shed their life's blood to maintain. Freedom, as we know it today, is so rare and so precious that President Ezra Taft Benson has commented: "Look back in retrospect on almost six thousand years of human history! Freedom's moments have been infrequent and exceptional. We must appreciate that we live in one of history's most exceptional moments—in a nation and a time of unprecedented freedom. Freedom as we know it has been experienced by perhaps less than 1 percent of the human family." (*Ensign,* September 1987, p. 6.)

Less than 1 percent of the human family has ever experienced what you and I have today! What a precious responsibility we have to maintain this freedom so truth may go to every nation, kindred, tongue, and people!

We cannot be satisfied to help preserve it for the Latter-day Saints only. We must fight for the rights of all men to worship God in their own way, even if it differs from what we know to be true. Joseph Smith said:

> The Saints can testify whether I am willing to lay down my life for my brethren. If it has been demonstrated that I have been willing to die for a "Mormon," I am bold to declare before Heaven that I am just as ready to die in defending the rights of a Presbyterian, a Baptist, or a good man of any other denomination; for the same principle which would trample upon the rights of the Latter-day Saints would trample upon the rights of the Roman

Catholics, or of any other denominations who may be un-
popular and too weak to defend themselves. (*Teachings of
the Prophet Joseph Smith,* comp. Joseph Fielding Smith [Salt
Lake City: Deseret Book Co., 1976], p. 313.)

The preservation of freedom can only come by living
righteously and doing all we can to merit the Lord's
blessings. "Our Constitution," said John Adams, first vice-
president and second president of the United States,
"was made only for a moral and religious people. It is
wholly inadequate to the government of any other." (As
quoted by John R. Howe, Jr., *The Changing Political Thought
of John Adams* [Princeton, N.J.: Princeton University Press,
1966], p. 185; as cited in *Ensign,* September 1987, p. 10.)

How are we doing as a country? as a community? as a
family? as an individual? Are we shaking "at the appearance of sin"? (2 Nephi 4:31.) Or, are we running to it,
eating, drinking, and being merry, hoping somehow that
God in his mercy will "beat us with a few stripes" and at
last save us in his kingdom? (See 2 Nephi 28:7–8.)

The present Constitution of the United States will not
work for a people who are not moral and righteous. If we
choose to run to sin rather than from it, it will destroy
not only our dreams and visions but ourselves and our
country.

What must we do then to preserve and keep this precious, fragile gift of freedom? President Benson has taught:

For the past two centuries, those who do not prize freedom have chipped away at our Constitution until today we
face a crisis of great dimensions. We are fast approaching
that moment prophesied by Joseph Smith when he said:

"Even this nation will be on the very verge of crum-
bling to pieces and tumbling to the ground, and when the
Constitution is upon the brink of ruin, this people will be

the staff upon which the nation shall lean, and they shall bear the Constitution away from the very verge of destruction."

Will we be prepared? Will we be among those who will "bear the Constitution away from the very verge of destruction"? If we desire to be numbered among those who will, here are some things we must do. (*Ensign,* September 1987, pp. 10–11.)

President Benson then listed four items that must be done:

1. "We must be righteous and moral."
2. "We must learn the principles of the Constitution and then abide by its precepts."
3. "We must become involved in civic affairs."
4. "We must make our influence felt by our vote, our letters, and our advice." (Ibid., p. 11.)

Before we briefly discuss each of these four items, let us ponder the wise words of King Benjamin: "And see that all these things are done in wisdom and order; for it is not requisite that a man should run faster than he has strength . . . ; therefore, all things must be done in order" (Mosiah 4:27). As we proceed to preserve our freedom of religion, it is critical that we not become alarmists or fanatics. Remember Elder Packer's wise counsel that when we try to force spiritual things, we open ourselves up to be deceived:

It is not wise to wrestle with the revelations with such insistence as to demand immediate answers or blessings to your liking. You cannot force spiritual things. Such words as compel, coerce, constrain, pressure, demand, do not describe our privileges with the Spirit. You can no more force the Spirit to respond than you can force a bean to sprout, or an egg to hatch before it's time. You can create a climate to foster growth, nourish, and protect; but you cannot force or compel: you must await the growth.

Do not be impatient to gain great spiritual knowledge. Let it grow, help it grow, but do not force it or you will open the way to be misled. . . .

Be ever on guard lest you be deceived by inspiration from an unworthy source. You can be given false spiritual messages. There are counterfeit angels. (See Moro. 7:17.) Be careful lest you be deceived, for the devil may come disguised as an angel of light.

The spiritual part of us and the emotional part of us are so closely linked that it is possible to mistake an emotional impulse for something spiritual. We occasionally find people who receive what they assume to be spiritual promptings from God, when those promptings are either centered in the emotions or are from the adversary. (*Ensign,* January 1983, p. 53, 55–56.)

Alma wisely counseled his son Shiblon to be bold but not overbearing and to bridle all his passions so that he might be filled with love (see Alma 38:12). We are to be filled with love, not a fanatical war cry! With this caution, let us briefly explore each of President Benson's four points.

1. *We must be righteous and moral.* The doing of simple, basic things such as searching the scriptures daily, praying daily, and following the prophets is the safest course to righteousness and morality. *Scriptures, prayers,* and *prophets* ought to be our bywords. (Each of these items will be discussed in later chapters.) Without these, even the ancients would not have remained faithful. Alma illustrated this point in an address to his sons:

I say unto you, my sons, were it not for these things, which have been kept and preserved by the hand of God, that we might read and understand of his mysteries, and have his commandments always before our eyes, that even our fathers would have dwindled in unbelief, and we should have been like unto our brethren, the Lamanites, who know nothing concerning these things, or even do not believe them when they are taught them, because of the traditions of their fathers, which are not correct (Mosiah 1:5).

There is no way to always remember God's commandments if we do not have the words of Christ always before our eyes. The converted Lamanites remained faithful all the days of their lives because they prayed, followed prophets, and heeded the words of the holy scriptures:

> And behold, ye do know of yourselves, for ye have witnessed it, that as many of them as are brought to the knowledge of the truth, and to know of the wicked and abominable traditions of their fathers, and are led to believe the holy scriptures, yea, the prophecies of the holy prophets, which are written, which leadeth them to faith on the Lord, and unto repentance, which faith and repentance bringeth a change of heart unto them—
>
> Therefore, as many as have come to this, ye know of yourselves are firm and steadfast in the faith, and in the thing wherewith they have been made free. (Helaman 15:7–8.)

Doing these simple things led to faith, which led to repentance, which led to a change of heart, which allowed them to "have been made free."

President Benson has said: "We must live the gospel principles—all of them. We have no right to expect a higher degree of morality from those who represent us than what we ourselves exhibit. To live a higher law means we will not seek to receive what we have not earned by our own labor. It means we will remember that government owes us nothing. It means we will keep the laws of the land. It means we will look to God as our Lawgiver and the Source of our liberty." (*Ensign,* September 1987, p. 11.)

2. *We must learn the principles of the Constitution and then abide by its precepts.*

Perhaps one reason why the Constitution is so misunderstood is that so few have read it. How many of us recognize when a law is constitutionally unsound? Can we really defend it?

Abraham Lincoln taught: "Let [the Constitution] be taught in schools, in seminaries, and in colleges; let it be written in primers, spelling-books, and in almanacs; let it be preached from the pulpit, proclaimed in legislative halls, and enforced in courts of justice. And, in short, let it become the political religion of the nation." (*Complete Works of Abraham Lincoln,* ed. John G. Nicolay and John Hay, 12 vols. [New York: Francis D. Tandy Co., 1905], 1:43.)

3. *We must become involved in civic affairs.* History books, as well as scriptures, are filled with stories of human suffering. When the wicked have been allowed to rule, the people mourn. Almost any current newspaper gives detailed, daily accounts of the oppression, suffering, and desperate conditions of many people in many lands. Much of this suffering results from the unrighteous dominion of a wicked ruler. The Lord told the Prophet Joseph Smith: "I, the Lord God, make you free, therefore ye are free indeed; and the law also maketh you free. Nevertheless, when the wicked rule the people mourn." (D&C 98:8–9.)

The Lord then declared what must be done in order to avoid the mourning: "Wherefore, honest men and wise men should be sought for diligently, and good men

and wise men ye should observe to uphold; otherwise
whatsoever is less than these cometh of evil" (D&C
98:10). Thus, according to the Lord, the men and
women who represent us must have three basic qualities:
they must be good, wise, and honest.

Our duty as citizens is to see that those elected to
public office possess all three of these qualities—good-
ness, wisdom, and honesty. President Benson has said,
"As citizens of this republic, we cannot do our duty and
be idle spectators" (*Ensign,* September 1987, p. 11). We
must do all we can to be a part of the process that
chooses our leaders. We cannot ignore history or the
scriptural accounts of wicked leaders and their negative
influences on the people.

King Mosiah proposed to his people a form of government that would allow the electing of judges rather than
having kings:

> Now I say unto you, that because all men are not just it
> is not expedient that ye should have a king or kings to rule
> over you.
>
> For behold, how much iniquity doth one wicked king
> cause to be committed, yea, and what great destruction!
>
> Yea, remember king Noah, his wickedness and his
> abominations, and also the wickedness and abominations
> of his people. Behold what great destruction did come
> upon them; and also because of their iniquities they were
> brought into bondage. . . .
>
> And behold, now I say unto you, ye cannot dethrone
> an iniquitous king save it be through much contention,
> and the shedding of much blood.
>
> For behold, he has his friends in iniquity, and he keep-
> eth his guards about him; and he teareth up the laws of
> those who have reigned in righteousness before him; and
> he trampleth under his feet the commandments of God;
>
> And he enacteth laws, and sendeth them forth among

his people, yea, laws after the manner of his own wickedness; and whosoever doth not obey his laws he causeth to be destroyed; and whosoever doth rebel against him he will send his armies against them to war, and if he can he will destroy them; and thus an unrighteous king doth pervert the ways of all righteousness. (Mosiah 29:16–18, 21–23.)

One night while watching the evening news on television, our youngest daughter began to cry. She watched a man from the former Yugoslavia browsing for food. The man with tattered clothing and a look of starvation on his face appeared hopeless in his quest for an evening meal. The commentator was describing the terrible poverty, death, and destruction that had resulted from the civil war between the Bosnians and the Serbs. As the indelible scenes of starvation and dying continued, our little daughter asked some soul-stirring questions. She wanted to know why Jesus didn't feed them. She cried, "Why can't they have the apples we picked at the welfare farm? Why can't we get a plane and bring them here so they can eat?"

She wept. I didn't have a very good answer for a five-year-old. I tried to explain. She didn't understand. It is very complicated, I'm sure, but I must wonder whether the people were suffering partly as the result of wicked leaders.

In his journal, President Benson described his experience in wartorn Europe shortly after the ending of World War II:

"People walking about in the ruins," he recorded, "seem almost as tho they were from another world. My heart grows heavy and my eyes fill with tears as I picture in my mind's eyes these scenes of horror and destruction. . . ."

Then it was on to Berlin. What he found there was in-describable. Miles of the city lay in utter waste. "Drove through once beautiful Berlin," he wrote the first night. "The wreckage . . . cannot possibly be understood unless seen. My soul rebels as I attempt to describe it. Truly war is hell in all its fury."

Months later, after witnessing dozens of similar scenarios, he wrote to Flora, "I'm so grateful you and the children can be spared the views of the terrible ravages of war. I fear I'll never be able to erase them from my memory."

. . . His journal observations are descriptive: "I witnessed scenes that seemed almost outside this world. . . . I saw the pomp and beauty of once proud Berlin at one time heralded by God-less leaders as the product of the 'master race' that would throw the principles of Christianity out the window and conquer the world by force, now a mass of sad wreckage. . . . I smelled the odor of decaying, human bodies. . . . I saw old men and women with small hatchets eagerly digging at tree stumps and roots in an effort to get scraps of fuel and then pulling them home for miles on anything that would roll. . . ."

Some things were even more frightening. Dachau, where the Americans saw the crematorium where 238,000 Jews were exterminated, was one of them. "The scenes and statistics given made us shudder to realize how far men will go in evil and sin when they discard the eternal truths of the gospel," Ezra wrote in his journal. . . .

In Warsaw Elder Benson and his companion stayed at the Polonia Hotel in a small room shared with seven other men. The pillage and devastation they saw seemed almost too much to bear. Ezra wrote to Flora, "As one walks about the city the most sickening odors meet you from debris, dead bodies in the ruins and filth. Because of the lack of sanitary facilities the people generally are filthy. . . . Cripples are everywhere. . . . One feels so helpless amidst it all, that you find yourself wanting to leave or shut yourself from it in your room." . . .

Ezra recorded in his journal: "We listened to the most harrowing accounts of the dastardly deeds of Russian soldiers. . . . Women and even little girls . . . were ravaged. . . . Cases were reported where as many as 10 soldiers one after the other forced relations with young girls . . . and in some cases while parents looked on at the point of a bayonet. . . . Never in all my life have I heard such terrors, many of which included coldblooded murder of husbands as their wives looked on helplessly." . . .

"The aftermath of war is usually worse than the actual physical combat. Everywhere there is the suffering of old people, innocent women and children. Economies are broken down, the spirits of people crushed, men and women bewildered. . . . It is a saddening thing to see people who have lost their freedom." (Sheri L. Dew, *Ezra Taft Benson: A Biography* [Salt Lake City: Deseret Book, 1987], pp. 210–12, 221–23, 227.)

We must do all we can to prevent atrocities like this from happening ever again. When people lose their freedom temporally or spiritually, the heavens weep. The great prophet Enoch taught that when people suffer, Satan laughs—and our Father and his Son weep:

And he beheld Satan; and he had a great chain in his hand, and it veiled the whole face of the earth with darkness; and he looked up and laughed, and his angels rejoiced. . . .

And it came to pass that the God of Heaven looked upon the residue of the people, and he wept; and Enoch bore record of it, saying: How is it that the heavens weep, and shed forth their tears as the rain upon the mountains?
. . .

The Lord said unto Enoch: Behold these thy brethren; they are the workmanship of mine own hands, and I gave unto them their knowledge, in the day I created them; and in the Garden of Eden, gave I unto man his agency. . . .

. . . And the whole heavens shall weep over them, even
all the workmanship of mine hands; wherefore should not
the heavens weep, seeing these shall suffer? (Moses 7:26,
28, 32, 37.)

From these verses it appears that when the Lord's
children suffer and choose not to return home to God,
the heavens weep. Should we not do all in our power to
help relieve human suffering, to stop the tears of heaven
from falling "as the rain upon the mountains?"

4. *We must make our influence felt by our vote, our letters,
and our advice.* It is important for us to be wisely informed
concerning the issues at hand. We ought to be women
and "men that [have] understanding of the times, to
know what Israel ought to do" (1 Chronicles 12:32). We
must, as President Benson has taught, "take part in local
precinct meetings and select delegates who will truly represent our feelings" (*Ensign,* September 1987, p. 11).

As mentioned at the beginning of this chapter, countless millions have given their very life's blood to maintain
and preserve freedom. It may yet cost us much more
blood before we are through.

3

Freedom Isn't Free

1940 to 1945 brought much sorrow to the small, central Utah town where my mother and father were raised. Spanish Fork was not much different than most rural American towns during the early 1940s. One of the only differences was an unusually high death rate of servicemen during the Second World War. In Spanish Fork, very few lives were untouched. Almost everyone in town lost a family member or friend to the cause of freedom. My family was no exception.

To this day, my father feels deeply the loss of his cousin "Big Chris," Allen Christianson. "Big Chris" was flying in a P-38 in North Africa; one day his plane collided with a B-17 bomber while landing. Chris did not survive the crash. Each Memorial Day I walk with my dad to Chris's grave and place flowers near his headstone. Each year I hear the same story and see the same sorrow in my father's eyes as he recounts what happened and remembers the good times they had before the war separated them.

Each year as we drive into the cemetery, we gaze at the many, many white crosses positioned in dozens of straight rows. Each cross honors a serviceman or woman from Spanish Fork who gave his or her life for freedom or served in the armed forces and died later of other causes.

Positioned in those rows are two crosses that have very special significance to my mother's family. These crosses bear the names of her two older brothers, Franklin and Ralph Pinegar. Franklin was killed aboard the USS *Walk,* a naval destroyer, and Ralph served on the USS *Talladega,* in the South Pacific. Ralph did not die until the 1970s, but the two brothers' lives were very much entwined in January of 1945.

Franklin served as an officer, and Ralph was a signalman. Both of their ships were engaged in the battle of the Lingayen Gulf.

The *Talladega* was a troop ship trying to land troops on a beach, and the *Walk* was a destroyer in a fleet of American ships providing protection for the troops so they could successfully take the beach and fulfill their mission.

The casualty rate for those landing on the beach from the troop ships was extremely high. All aboard knew that the chances of survival were slim to none. However, they bravely attempted to fulfill their missions in order to provide freedom for future generations. On a typical beach landing, the casualty rate could be as high as 85 percent of the first wave of soldiers and marines, and 50 percent of the second wave. It is difficult to imagine what went through the minds of these valiant young men as they contemplated giving their lives so others might be free. Perhaps these sobering words of the Savior filled their minds and hearts: "Greater love hath no man than this, that a man lay down his life for his friends" (John 15:13).

The battle Franklin and Ralph were engaged in had been going on for some six days. The Japanese had been making air strikes, and the USS *Walk* had done everything it could to protect the *Talladega* and the other ships. On the sixth day of the battle, six Japanese suicide bombers attempted an attack. Five were shot down before they reached any ships; the sixth, evidently realizing it would never reach the *Talladega* or other troop ships, decided to blow up the *Walk*. As the pilot flew his plane towards the deck of the *Walk*, Franklin stood on the bridge watching a young teenage gunner firing in the direction of the oncoming plane. The tracer bullets were not being fired anywhere near the oncoming plane, and Franklin knew that if the plane released its bomb and hit the ship, the entire crew could be killed, leaving one less destroyer to protect the troop ships.

In an instant, Franklin did his duty as an officer: he ran from the bridge to the antiaircraft gun, threw the young soldier down some stairs to safety, and began firing at the suicide bomber.

The pilot was shot and killed before he could release his bomb. However, Franklin could not stop the plane from hitting the ship. He kept firing to the very end. The plane hit the ship right where Franklin was standing, killing him instantly. The ship survived because the bomb on the plane did not explode. The young teenage gunner survived because he had been thrown to safety. Ralph and the *Talladega* survived because the suicide planes never reached their decks. But Franklin lost his life in preserving others' lives. He died a hero—a true hero! He was buried at sea, and none of his family or friends ever saw his remains. His beautiful wife, daughter, and unborn son were left without their hero so others might be free. He fulfilled the words of the Savior and laid down his life for his friends. He died not only for his friends but also for his brother Ralph on the *Talladega*. He not only laid down his life for Ralph but for you and me as well.

Each time I enter the Spanish Fork cemetery, I think of these events. Of course, I can't share all that happened and how the lives of the teenage gunner and my Uncle Ralph turned out, but I can say that their lives were forever altered that January day in 1945.

The lives of my grandparents, my mother, my uncles and aunt, and now yours and mine, cannot and never will be the same.

Are we living righteous and moral lives so we can show our gratitude for all the Franklins who have willingly given their lives so you and I could worship God in our own way? Or have we given our freedom and its cost very little thought and appreciation?

Again, freedom isn't free. The cost is always life and blood. We must accept the freedom offered, not only the temporal freedom given us by our fellowman but also the spiritual freedom given us by God our Father and his Eternal Son. Never is freedom possible without death. Never. Even our choosing to come to earth and have the agency we treasure has its price. It is death. All mortal men must die. That is the agreement. We come to earth and are free to choose for ourselves, but the price for this freedom is that every man, woman, and child must die. Mortality costs us our lives to be free!

Freedom of religion, freedom of press, freedom of speech, and many other types of freedom have cost us the lives of countless valiant men and women. The price for spiritual freedom is no different.

Nearly two thousand years ago, the greatest blood

that ever coursed through earthly veins was spilt on the floor of a dusty garden and on a cross so that you and I could be forgiven of our sins and live forever. To put it simply, the greatest sacrifice in the history of this universe, and the highest price ever paid for anything, were given for you and me. Through the atoning sacrifice of Jesus Christ we were each bought for a price. That price was the life of the Son of God.

Yes, we were bought. The price paid was so high that most of us have but a faint notion at best as to its significance. The Apostle Paul taught us well on this subject: "What? know ye not that your body is the temple of the Holy Ghost which is in you, which ye have of God, and ye are not your own? For ye are bought with a price: therefore glorify God in your body, and in your spirit, which are God's." (1 Corinthians 6:19–20.)

When considering this ultimate act of love, my heartstrings are wrenched with pain, yet my eyes cry tears of joy. My soul sings out the words, "Oh, it is wonderful that he should care for me / Enough to die for me" ("I Stand All Amazed," *Hymns,* no. 193).

Christ himself gave the Prophet Joseph Smith a brief glimpse of what transpired that night:

> For behold, I, God, have suffered these things for all, that they might not suffer if they would repent;
> But if they would not repent they must suffer even as I;
> Which suffering caused myself, even God, the greatest of all, to tremble because of pain, and to bleed at every pore, and to suffer both body and spirit—and would that I might not drink the bitter cup, and shrink—
> Nevertheless, glory be to the Father, and I partook and finished my preparations unto the children of men. (D&C 19:16–19.)

In the Gospel of Luke we also learn that Jesus' suffering was so intense that an angel was sent to strengthen him: "Father, if thou be willing, remove this cup from me: nevertheless not my will, but thine, be done. And there appeared an angel unto him from heaven, strengthening him. And being in an agony he prayed more earnestly: and his sweat was as it were great drops of blood falling down to the ground." (Luke 22:42–44.)

Can any of us understand such love and devotion? "The thought makes reason stare" ("O My Father," *Hymns,* no. 292).

This agony in the garden was not the end of his suffering. After this experience, our Lord was taken like a criminal and stripped naked. He was beaten, spit upon, mocked, scourged, slapped across the face, and crucified on a cross between two thieves. All this he endured without offering any resistance. And at the end, he pleaded with his Father and our Father to "forgive them; for they know not what they do" (Luke 23:34).

Why did he pay such a price? Why do we oftentimes, along with the world, reject his ultimate sacrifice? Perhaps the words of the prophet Nephi answer these two questions best: "And the world, because of their iniquity, shall judge him to be a thing of naught; wherefore they scourge him, and he suffereth it; and they smite him, and he suffereth it. Yea, they spit upon him, and he suffereth it, because of his loving kindness and his long-suffering towards the children of men." (1 Nephi 19:9.)

Let us not think of this price as a "thing of naught." Let us not trample under our feet the Holy One of Israel (see Alma 5:53; Helaman 12:2).

He called us his "friends" if we do whatsoever he commands us (see John 15:14). He lived as he taught. He showed us the greatest love of all. He gave his life so that we might be free! Can we not be brave in this world and accept this most wonderful of all offerings? Yes! The answer is yes! We can be brave, and we can "come unto Christ, and lay hold upon every good gift, and touch not the evil gift, nor the unclean thing" (Moroni 10:30).

4

God Needs Brave Sons and Daughters

Elder Henry B. Eyring of the First Quorum of the Seventy tells a moving story about his father, Dr. Henry Eyring, that has had a profound impact in my life. Dr. Eyring lay in a hospital bed suffering from bone cancer. On one occasion, he attempted to climb out of bed to kneel on the floor and pray. Elder Eyring asked him why he needed to get out of bed in order to pray. His father responded that he needed to ask Father in Heaven a very significant question that required that he kneel.

Elder Eyring asked what was so important that it couldn't be asked from the hospital bed. His father responded that he wanted to ask the Lord why he was allowing him to suffer so terribly when he had been so faithful all his life. Why, as his life came to a close, was there so much suffering when he had lived so righteously?

Understandingly, Elder Eyring did not stop his father from praying on his knees. When the prayer was finished and Dr. Eyring was back in bed, his son asked if he had received the answer to his question concerning his suffering. His answer was one that was not only thought provoking but life altering.

He said: "Yes, son, I did receive an answer. I learned that God needs brave sons. And I must be brave!"

What an incredible lesson! God needs brave sons, and he needs brave daughters, and we must be brave! If ever there was a need for us to be brave, it is now! How can we dream dreams and have visions if we don't have the courage to live the gospel? How can we maintain our freedom both temporally and spiritually if we are not brave enough to be righteous and moral?

Of course it's not easy. Being a disciple of Jesus Christ has always required bravery! As our world darkens and the enemy of all righteousness seems to be winning on every battle front, we must be brave! We must stand for truth and righteousness. We must hold up that light which is Christ: "Therefore, hold up your light that it may shine unto the world. Behold I am the light which ye shall hold up—that which ye have seen me do." (3 Nephi 18:24.) We must be brave.

President Spencer W. Kimball wrote:

Whoever said that sin was not fun? Whoever claimed that Lucifer was not handsome, persuasive, easy, friendly? Sin is attractive and desirable. Transgression wears elegant gowns and sparkling apparel. It is highly perfumed; it has attractive features, a soft voice. It is found in educated circles and sophisticated groups. It provides sweet and comfortable luxuries. Sin is easy and has a big company of pleasant companions. It promises immunity from restrictions, temporary freedoms. It can momentarily satisfy hunger, thirst, desire, urges, passions, wants without immediate paying the price. But, it begins tiny and grows to monumental proportions—drop by drop, inch by inch. . . .

Would a frequent housecleaning be in order for all of us?

I may not be able to eliminate pornographic trash, but my family and I need not buy or view it.

I may not be able to close disreputable businesses, but I can stay away from areas of questioned honor and ill repute.

I may not be able to greatly reduce the divorces of the land or save all broken homes and frustrated children, but I can keep my own home a congenial one, my marriage happy, my home a heaven, and my children well adjusted.

I may not be able to stop the growing claims to freedom from laws based on morals, or change all opinions regarding looseness in sex and growing perversions, but I can guarantee devotion to all high ideals and standards in my own home, and I can work toward giving my own family a happy, interdependent spiritual life. (*Faith Precedes the Miracle* [Salt Lake City: Deseret Book Co., 1978], pp. 229, 247).

Yes, the world may appear to be attractive and enticing, but we cannot ever forget these words of Elder Neal A. Maxwell: "Someday, when we look back on mortality, we will see that many of the things that seemed to matter so much at the moment will be seen not to have mattered at all. And the eternal things will be seen to have mattered even more than the most faithful of the Saints imagined." (*Even As I Am* [Salt Lake City: Deseret Book Co., 1982], p. 104). To stay true to the "eternal things," we can be—indeed we must be—brave! Our Father needs us.

Elder L. Tom Perry of the Quorum of the Twelve Apostles has said: "We live today in a world so full of choices. Television offers both the good and the bad. Bookstores are full of publications offering the right and the wrong. Very few movies are worthy of seeing because of the profanity, violence, and immorality that fill them.

Advertising is full of enticements to lead us to violate the Word of Wisdom. Some music, with its monotonous rhythms, beats illicit thoughts into our heads." (*Ensign,* November 1993, p. 67.)

Elder Perry then asks us to consider the wonderful counsel given by President Spencer W. Kimball concerning our deciding to decide. He quotes President Kimball:

> Now may I make a recommendation? Develop discipline of self so that, more and more, you do not have to decide and redecide what you will do when you are confronted with the same temptation time and time again. You need only to decide some things once. How great a blessing it is to be free of agonizing over and over again regarding a temptation. To do such is time-consuming and very risky.
>
> Likewise, my dear young friends, the positive things you will want to accomplish need be decided upon only once—like going on a mission and living worthily in order to get married in the temple—and then all other decisions related to these goals can fall into line. Otherwise, each consideration is risky, and each equivocation may result in error. There are some things Latter-day Saints do and other things we just don't do. The sooner you take a stand, the taller you will be! (*President Kimball Speaks Out* [Salt Lake City: Deseret Book Co., 1981], p. 94.)

It is time to take a stand. It is time to stand taller in righteousness than ever before. As Elder Glenn L. Pace has taught:

> I believe the time has come for all of us to feast on the fruit of our own testimony as opposed to the testimony of another person. The testimony of which I speak is much deeper than knowing the Church is true. We need to progress to the point of knowing we are true to the

Church. We also need to increase our capacity to receive personal revelation. It is one thing to receive a witness that Joseph Smith saw God and Christ. It is quite another to have spiritual self-confidence in your ability to receive the revelation to which you are entitled. (*Ensign,* November 1992, p. 11.)

Again, we need to progress to the point of knowing more than that the Church is true, but that we are true to the Church. Most of us know that the Church is true. I believe that. Even when we doubt and wonder, our blood, the blood of Israel, cries out to us that the Church is true.

If, for example, you attend nearly any ward in the Church on fast Sunday, you will likely hear several children bear their testimonies. Most are completely sincere when they say almost the same words that every other child says while bearing testimony. "I know the Church is true. I love my mom and dad."

At one point in my life, I was a little uncomfortable hearing this seemingly rote testimony. Then, I learned a great lesson from our six-year-old daughter. After fast meeting one Sunday afternoon, she came to me and said, "Bishop, I'd like to bear my testimony next fast Sunday. Do you want to hear it?"

Of course I indicated that I did. She then stood on the arm of the couch in the family room and started with a great deal of confidence: "I know the Church is true. I love my mom and dad. I love my grandparents. I love Jesus and the Book of Mormon."

When she finished, I responded very positively and then tried to counsel her a little. I said, "That's great, sweetheart. But why don't you say something like 'I know that God lives. Jesus is the Christ. The Book of Mormon is true. Joseph Smith was a true prophet.'"

Tears welled up in her eyes, her bottom lip started to quiver, and she jumped off the couch, ran upstairs, and slammed the door to her bedroom. I quickly and apologetically ran upstairs and tried to quiet her sobs. She would not be comforted. Finally she blurted out, "You didn't like my testimony!" I tried to assure her that I loved her testimony, but then she taught me the lesson. She said, "You just want me to say what you want me to say, not what I feel in here!" patting her hand upon her chest.

I was stunned. She was right. As I held her in my arms, I realized that what she really knew at her stage of life was that the Church was true, she loved her mom and dad, and she loved Jesus. That's where she was. Those words were her sincere testimony.

You and I need to progress to the point of being true to the Church and to being able to have the spiritual self-confidence needed to receive the revelation to which we are entitled. The Savior, in answer to the pleadings of Joseph Smith from Liberty Jail, said:

> Let thy bowels also be full of charity towards all men, and to the household of faith, and let virtue garnish thy thoughts unceasingly; then shall thy confidence wax strong in the presence of God; and the doctrine of the priesthood shall distil upon thy soul as the dews from heaven.
>
> The Holy Ghost shall be thy constant companion, and thy scepter an unchanging scepter of righteousness and truth; and thy dominion shall be an everlasting dominion, and without compulsory means it shall flow unto thee forever and ever. (D&C 121:45–46.)

Spiritual confidence comes from exercising charity and letting "virtue garnish our thoughts unceasingly." Perhaps a brief story can illustrate this point.

While speaking at a Know Your Religion series in New Mexico, I had a moving experience. I had given an hour and a half lecture on "The Book of Mormon and Modern Man." When the lecture was finished, I was introduced to a man who worked as a researcher at New Mexico State University. He was not a Latter-day Saint but was very polite and had several questions as a result of my lecture. He had come with a friend who was a member of the Church. He had brought his Bible, and it was obvious that he intended to use it to show me why the Book of Mormon was not necessary.

After a brief introduction, he asked if I had some time to answer some questions. I assured him I did, and our discussion began.

He commented that he knew we had an article of faith that declared we believed the Bible to be the word of God as far as it was translated correctly. I quickly interjected that we also believed the Book of Mormon to be the word of God. He then asked: "Could you please show me which scriptures in the Bible are translated incorrectly?"

After silently gasping and praying for the Spirit to assist me, I thought of an answer. I asked, "Before I show you any specific scriptures, may I discuss the coming forth of the Bible first?" He agreed that that would be an appropriate place to begin. After about ten minutes of explanation concerning the history of the Bible, he didn't feel like I was answering his question. I responded, "Oh, but I am, and until we understand the history of the Bible and its coming forth, it will be very difficult to understand why some of it is translated incorrectly." He agreed. We finally discussed a few specific scriptures, but by then the Spirit was touching his heart and he began to ask many other questions that had evidently troubled him for some time. He asked about plural marriage,

Blacks and the priesthood, women and the priesthood, and several other sensitive issues. I answered many of them from modern scripture, which didn't please him. I then told him there were really only two questions he ever had to resolve when it came to religion. First, is there a God? Second, is the Book of Mormon true? He felt that was not only idealistic but far too simplified. I paraphrased Doctrine and Covenants 20:8–12, which reads:

> And gave him power from on high, by the means which were before prepared, to translate the Book of Mormon;
> Which contains a record of a fallen people, and the fulness of the gospel of Jesus Christ to the Gentiles and to the Jews also;
> Which was given by inspiration, and is confirmed to others by the ministering of angels, and is declared unto the world by them—
> Proving to the world that the holy scriptures are true, and that God does inspire men and call them to his holy work in this age and generation, as well as in generations of old;
> Thereby showing that he is the same God yesterday, today, and forever. Amen.

I tried to help him understand that a major purpose for the Book of Mormon is to prove to the world that the Bible is true. It is in truth a second witness for Jesus Christ. We then reasoned that if the Book of Mormon were true, then Jesus truly was the Son of God, that he did indeed have a glorified and perfected body of flesh and bones. If the book were true, Christ was, in reality, a separate being from the Father, and he does still communicate with mortal men. We reasoned further that if the Book of Mormon were true, then Joseph Smith was a true prophet. If Joseph Smith was a true prophet, The

Church of Jesus Christ of Latter-day Saints is the only true church on the earth. If this Church is true, the First Presidency and the members of the Quorum of the Twelve Apostles truly are prophets, seers, and revelators, and we had better follow them.

I thought the reasoning process was going smoothly until he said abruptly, "I have the Bible and that's all I need! The Bible is final! It is infallible! It is forever!"

Memories of a summer school class with Dr. Stephen E. Robinson came into my mind. Dr. Robinson had had a similar experience, so I answered with his question: "Where in the Bible does it say that?" He responded with a stutter and then with an admission that he wasn't sure. However, he said he was sure that it was somewhere in the Bible. I explained that I had read both the Old and the New Testament a number of times and didn't recall reading that anywhere. Then the inspiration came. A thought came into my mind to open the Book of Mormon and read parts of the twenty-ninth chapter of 2 Nephi. It made me very nervous. The butterflies that fluttered in the pit of my stomach felt like eagles! He agreed to read it and was quite shocked with what he read. In a vision of the latter days Nephi wrote:

> But behold, there shall be many—at that day when I shall proceed to do a marvelous work among them, that I may remember my covenants which I have made unto the children of men, that I may set my hand again the second time to recover my people, which are of the house of Israel;
>
> And also, that I may remember the promises which I have made unto thee, Nephi, and also unto thy father, that I would remember your seed; and that the words of your seed should proceed forth out of my mouth unto your seed; and my words shall hiss forth unto the ends of the earth, for a standard unto my people, which are of the house of Israel;

And because my words shall hiss forth—many of the Gentiles shall say: A Bible! A Bible! We have got a Bible, and there cannot be any more Bible.

But thus saith the Lord God; O fools, they shall have a Bible; and it shall proceed forth from the Jews, mine ancient covenant people. And what thank they the Jews for the Bible which they receive from them? Yea, what do the Gentiles mean? Do they remember the travails, and the labors, and the pains of the Jews, and their diligence unto me, in bringing forth salvation unto the Gentiles? . . .

Thou fool, that shall say: A Bible, we have got a Bible, and we need no more Bible. Have ye obtained a Bible save it were by the Jews?

Know ye not that there are more nations than one? Know ye not that I, the Lord your God, have created all men, and that I remember those who are upon the isles of the sea; and that I rule in the heavens above and in the earth beneath; and I bring forth my word unto the children of men, yea, even upon all the nations of the earth?

Wherefore murmur ye, because that ye shall receive more of my word? Know ye not that the testimony of two nations is a witness unto you that I am God, that I remember one nation like unto another? Wherefore, I speak the same words unto one nation like unto another. And when the two nations shall run together the testimony of the two nations shall run together also.

And I do this that I may prove unto many that I am the same yesterday, today, and forever; and that I speak forth my words according to mine own pleasure. And because that I have spoken one word ye need not suppose that I cannot speak another; for my work is not yet finished; neither shall it be until the end of man, neither from that time henceforth and forever.

Wherefore, because that ye have a Bible ye need not suppose that it contains all my words; neither need ye suppose that I have not caused more to be written. (2 Nephi 29:1–4, 6–10.)

Never, without the spiritual confidence I had felt, would I have dared read something so straightforward to a nonmember. He said, "That sounds like what I just said." I agreed. I then put my arm around him as we walked to the parking lot. I bore my testimony and pleaded with him to prayerfully read the Book of Mormon. I let him know that he could know for himself that it was true. I have not heard from him since and have no idea if he accepted my invitation. However, the lesson is that I needed the spiritual self-confidence to discuss the scriptures of the Restoration with him and believe that the Lord would bless me in this great time of need. I needed to know more than just that the Church was true. You see, it wasn't possible to call a religion teacher and ask for the scripture chain on the Joseph Smith Translation that was covered in class. I am a religion teacher. I couldn't call my dad and ask for the answers. I am the dad. I couldn't call my bishop. Currently, I am my bishop. By being brave we can qualify to receive revelation in times of need.

Elder Pace commented further:

> Many of us take the blessings of the gospel for granted. It is as if we are passengers on the train of the Church, which has been moving forward gradually and methodically. Sometimes we have looked out the window and thought, "That looks kind of fun out there. This train is so restrictive." So we have jumped off and gone and played in the woods for a while. Sooner or later, we find it isn't as much fun as Lucifer makes it appear or we get critically injured, so we work our way back to the tracks and see the train ahead. With a determined sprint we catch up to it, breathlessly wipe the perspiration from our forehead, and thank the Lord for repentance.
>
> While on the train, we can see the world and some of

our own members outside laughing and having a great time. They taunt us and coax us to get off. Some throw logs and rocks on the tracks to try and derail it. Other members run alongside the tracks, and while they may never go play in the woods, they just can't seem to get on the train. Others try to run ahead and too often take the wrong turn.

I would propose that the luxury of getting on and off the train as we please is fading. The speed of the train is increasing. The woods are getting much too dangerous, and the fog and darkness are moving in.

Although our detractors might as well "stretch forth [their] puny arm[s] to stop the Missouri river in its decreed course, or to turn it up stream" (D&C 121:33) than to derail this train, they are occasionally successful in coaxing individuals off. With all the prophecies we have seen fulfilled, what great event are we awaiting prior to saying, "Count me in"? What more do we need to see or experience before we get on the train and stay on it until we reach our destination? It is time for a spiritual revival. It is time to dig down deep within ourselves and rekindle our own light. . . .

I make a special appeal to the youth. You will remain much safer and infinitely happier if you will place your energy into current obedience rather than saving it for future repentance. (*Ensign*, November 1992, pp. 11–12.)

We must get on the train of the Church and be brave enough to stay on it. We must gain our own testimony rather than always try to live on borrowed light. We must avoid the temptation to run ahead of the Brethren, and we must be brave enough to be obedient to their teachings. The Savior taught, "And the arm of the Lord shall be revealed; and the day cometh that they who will not hear the voice of the Lord, neither the voice of his servants, neither give heed to the words of the prophets and apostles, shall be cut off from among the people" (D&C 1:14).

These leaders who have been called of God "speak with a single, perfect heart which, I promise you, gives them an understanding of our times and of what the Church ought to do" (Monte J. Brough, *Ensign*, November 1993, p. 65).

Following living prophets and Apostles, as well as being brave sons and daughters of God, is not always easy. However, it is always right! Never before has God needed brave sons and brave daughters as he does now. Never has it been more vital to stand tall and straight for the cause of truth and righteousness as it is in these modern times. We can be strong and of good courage if we will keep our eyes riveted on the Savior and his ordained representatives. By so doing we can withstand any weapon used by the adversary as he so cunningly seeks to destroy our courage and strength as we stand as brave sons and daughters of Almighty God.

5

Withstanding
Sexual Pressure

Withstanding the sexual pressures of our day is an incredible challenge. It is not just a challenge for the young and inexperienced. It is a pressure most people face, regardless of age. However, it is a challenge that can be overcome when met with strength and courage. We must be brave sons and daughters of God, for it seems that Satan has unleashed every vile practice in order to destroy and blind those sons and daughters. Surely, "the mists of darkness" spoken of by Father Lehi and in which Satan performs his labors have descended over the earth as a thick blanket of confusion.

Elder Boyd K. Packer of the Quorum of the Twelve Apostles described modern sexual pressures this way:

> The rapid, sweeping deterioration of values is characterized by a preoccupation—even an obsession—with the procreative act. Abstinence before marriage and fidelity within it are openly scoffed at—marriage and parenthood

ridiculed as burdensome, unnecessary. Modesty, a virtue
of a refined individual or society, is all but gone.

The adversary is jealous toward all who have the power
to beget life. He cannot beget life; he is impotent. He and
those who followed him were cast out and forfeited the
right to a mortal body. His angels even begged to inhabit
the bodies of swine. (See Matt. 8:31.) And the revelations
tell us that "he seeketh that all men might be miserable
like unto himself." (2 Ne. 2:27). (*Ensign,* May 1992, p. 66.)

Isn't that last line perceptive? The purpose of sexual
pressure and similar temptations is to make us miserable!
Satan desires us to be sickeningly unhappy!

Elder Packer continues: "With ever fewer exceptions,
what we see and read and hear have the mating act as a
central theme. Censorship is forced offstage as a violation of individual freedom.

"That which should be absolutely private is disrobed
and acted out center stage. In the shadows backstage are
addiction, pornography, perversion, infidelity, abortion,
and—the saddest of them all—incest and molestation. In
company with them now is a plague of biblical propor-
tion. And all of them are on the increase." (Ibid.)

With so many voices in the world screaming at you to
abandon your standards of morality and come and join
in the party, how do you stand? Are you committed, determined, and straight? The purpose of this chapter is to
share principles that will help you to resist the temptations that come from every direction.

Many years ago I read an article by then Bishop
Vaughn J. Featherstone that has had a great influence on
me. I have used it often in sermons and speeches because its message is the key to withstanding the sexual
pressures all around us. The article centered on a story
about the son of King Louis XVI of France:

King Louis had been taken from his throne and impris-
oned. His young son, the prince, was taken by those who
dethroned the king. They thought that inasmuch as the
king's son was heir to the throne, if they could destroy him
morally, he would never realize the great and grand des-
tiny that life had bestowed upon him. [Sounds exactly like
Satan's plan for us today! Destroy our morals and we never
do realize who we are or why we're here.]

They took him to a community far away, and there
they exposed the lad to every filthy and vile thing that life
could offer. They exposed him to foods the richness of
which would quickly make him a slave to appetite. They
used vile language around him constantly. They exposed
him to lewd and lusting women. They exposed him to dis-
honor and distrust. He was surrounded 24 hours a day by
everything that could drag the soul of a man as low as one
could slip. For over six months he had this treatment—but
not once did the young lad buckle under pressure. Finally,
after intensive temptation, they questioned him. Why had
he not submitted himself to these things—why had he not
partaken? These things would provide pleasure, satisfy his
lusts, and were desirable; they were all his. The boy said, "I
cannot do what you ask for I was born to be a king." ("The
King's Son," *New Era,* November 1975, p. 35.)

What a heroic response! The prince would not give in
to all the pressures because he knew he had been born to
be a king! You and I are also born to be kings and
queens. Our Father is a King. He is the King of kings—
the King of all things. He is God.

My wife and I have all daughters, and we desire to re-
mind them of who they are and for what purpose they
were born, so hanging on the wall beside our front door
is a framed plaque that reads "I was born to be a queen."
Some may scoff and say that this approach to withstanding worldly sexual pressure is too idealistic or too simple.

But as far as I'm concerned, it is the "very key" to withstanding those pressures.

Elder Boyd K. Packer has also stated:

You are a child of God. He is the father of your spirit. Spiritually you are of noble birth, the offspring of the King of Heaven. Fix that truth in your mind and hold to it. However many generations in your mortal ancestry, no matter what race or people you represent, the pedigree of your spirit can be written on a single line. You are a child of God! . . .

Within your body is the power to beget life, to share in creation. The only legitimate expression of the power is within the covenant of marriage. The worthy use of it is the very key to your happiness. Do not use the power prematurely, not with anyone. The misuse of it cannot be made right by making it popular.

Your spirit operates through your mind, but cultivating your intellect is not enough. Reason alone will neither protect nor redeem you. Reason nourished by faith can do both. (*Ensign*, May 1989, p. 54.)

There has never been an idea more destructive to happiness or one that has produced more sorrow and pain and destroyed more families than the idea that we are not children of God but are instead only advanced animals that must follow and give in to every natural urge and desire.

With the knowledge that you are a son or daughter of the Heavenly King rooted firmly within you, you can understand the need for complete chastity. Then you will be fortified with the courage and strength to withstand the "mists of darkness" that shroud the world.

The First Presidency has declared: "A correct understanding of the divinely appointed roles of men and women will fortify all against sinful practices. Our only real safety, physically and spiritually, lies in keeping the Lord's commandments." (14 November 1991.)

This correct understanding includes comprehending why sexual intimacy is so sacred and why the Lord requires self-control and purity before marriage and full fidelity after marriage. We then begin to understand why the physical relationship between a husband and a wife can be beautiful and sacred. This relationship is ordained of God for two purposes: the procreation of children and the expression of love within a marriage (see *For the Strength of Youth* [Salt Lake City: The Church of Jesus Christ of Latter-day Saints, 1990], pp. 14–15).

I have often heard young people ask: "Why does a little piece of paper make such a difference? Why in one minute are sexual relations not okay and the next minute, after a brief ceremony, they are okay?"

Many seem to feel that as long as they are "safe" and a pregnancy does not occur or a disease is not contracted, everything is okay. You need to understand that having sexual relations outside of marriage is not wrong simply because a pregnancy may occur or because a deadly disease, like AIDS, may be contracted. Those are definitely two important reasons why you need to be morally clean, but they are not the major reasons. The most important reasons run far deeper, and if you understand them, that understanding will help you withstand sexual pressures.

1. One reason God is God is that he possesses the power to create and give life. He possesses a "continuation of the seeds forever and ever" (D&C 132:19). He has placed within his children the same power—a power we possess in a limited form here on earth and that he has promised he will bestow in eternity on those who keep his commandments. Obviously, there are many people who, because of physical limitations, cannot create life. But most human beings can participate in the act of creation.

To act as a creator simply requires permission from the Giver of the Law. The Lord has explained:

> And again, verily I say unto you, if a man marry a wife by my word, which is my law, and by the new and everlasting covenant, and it is sealed unto them by the Holy Spirit of promise, by him who is anointed, unto whom I have appointed this power and the keys of this priesthood; and it shall be said unto them—Ye shall come forth in the first resurrection; and if it be after the first resurrection, in the next resurrection; and shall inherit thrones, kingdoms, principalities, and powers, dominions, all heights and depths—then shall it be written in the Lamb's Book of Life, that he shall commit no murder whereby to shed innocent blood, and if ye abide in my covenant, and commit no murder whereby to shed innocent blood, it shall be done unto them in all things whatsoever my servant hath put upon them, in time, and through all eternity; and shall be of full force when they are out of the world; and they shall pass by the angels, and the gods, which are set there, to their exaltation and glory in all things, as hath been sealed upon their heads, which glory shall be a fulness and a continuation of the seeds forever and ever. . . .
>
> Verily, verily, I say unto you, except ye abide my law ye cannot attain to this glory." (D&C 132;19, 21.)

2. While describing the condition of his people to his son Moroni, the prophet Mormon painted a picture of the depths of depravity to which the Nephites and Lamanites had sunk. It sickens us to read how little they valued human life and how cruel they had become. Yet, in this depiction, a wonderful lesson on the value of chastity and virtue is taught:

> And the husbands and fathers of those women and children they have slain; and they feed the women upon

the flesh of their husbands, and the children upon the flesh of their fathers; and no water, save a little, do they give unto them.

And notwithstanding this great abomination of the Lamanites, it doth not exceed that of our people in Moriantum. For behold, many of the daughters of the Lamanites have they taken prisoners; and after depriving them of that which was most dear and precious above all things, which is chastity and virtue—

And after they had done this thing, they did murder them in a most cruel manner, torturing their bodies even unto death; and after they have done this, they devour their flesh like unto wild beasts, because of the hardness of their hearts; and they do it for a token of bravery. (Moroni 9:8–10.)

Why are chastity and virtue more "dear and precious" than "all things"? Why are they of more value than life itself? Because they are the very source of life! Thinking, breathing, feeling human beings are brought into existence through the magnificent act of procreation. Nevertheless, as Elder Packer has said: "The source of life is now relegated to the level of unwed pleasure, bought and sold and even defiled in satanic rituals. Children of God can willfully surrender to their carnal nature and, without remorse, defy the laws of morality and degrade themselves even below the beasts.

"If we pollute our fountains of life, there will be penalties 'exquisite' and 'hard to bear' (see D&C 19:15), more than all of the physical pleasure ever could be worth." (*Ensign*, May 1992, pp. 67–68.)

3. Alma told his son Corianton: "Know ye not, my son, that these things are an abomination in the sight of the Lord; yea, most abominable above all sins save it be the shedding of innocent blood or denying the Holy Ghost?" (Alma 39:5).

Why would the misuse of these sexual powers be next to murder in seriousness? When an individual murders someone, the murderer forces the victim's spirit out of his or her body. That leaves the body and spirit separated until the resurrection. The murderer has interfered with another's agency and has forced the murdered person into the spirit world, thus depriving the murdered person of any further earthly experience and leaving a wake of sorrow and pain for those who remain in mortality.

When two people misuse their creative powers and a pregnancy occurs outside a regularly constituted family, a spirit is forced to leave its premortal existence and enter into the newly created body. In this way too, an individual's agency is tampered with and God's plan is violated.

Because of eternal ramifications, the Lord has reserved the prerogative to decide the proper time for his children to either enter or leave mortality. It is God who "hath made of one blood all nations of men for to dwell on all the face of the earth, and hath determined the times before appointed, and the bounds of their habitation" (Acts 17:26). The Lord simply has forbidden the taking of spirits out of bodies and the bringing of spirits into bodies without his permission, saying: "Thou shalt love thy neighbor as thyself. Thou shalt not steal; neither commit adultery, nor kill, nor do anything like unto it" (D&C 59:6). Furthermore, he has reserved his most severe punishments for those who presume to trifle with the sanctity of life.

A marriage certificate is a permission slip, so to speak, from the Lord that allows us to participate with him in his plan to "multiply, and replenish the earth" (Moses 2:28), to provide bodies for his spirit children. And it is only in marriage that men and women are authorized so to act and to express their love in the most intimate ways.

4. We participate in the gospel of Jesus Christ by mak-

ing covenants. The covenants are entered into by participating in ordinances and thereby making promises, which we are asked to renew frequently in various ways. For example, by being baptized we "witness before [Christ] that [we] have entered into a covenant with him" (Mosiah 18:10) to take upon us his name, to always remember him, and to keep his commandments. Then, weekly, we renew that covenant by partaking of the sacrament (see D&C 20:77, 79).

The order, then, is to make a covenant, participate in an ordinance, and then renew the covenant. Should marriage, "the new and everlasting covenant" (D&C 132:19), be any different? We make a sacred covenant with our spouse to give ourselves completely to each other. We are sealed or married by proper authority (the ordinance). Then, we renew the covenant we have made to give all that we have and to be "one flesh." How do we renew the covenant? One way is to express our love by giving ourselves completely to our spouse in a sexual relationship. As Jeffrey R. Holland has said, the sexual union between a husband and a wife is in a sense a sacrament, or renewal of the marriage covenant (See "Of Souls, Symbols, and Sacraments," *Brigham Young University 1987–88 Devotional and Fireside Speeches* [Provo: Brigham Young University Press, 1988], pp. 73–85).

The violation of the law of chastity, then, is a violation of one of the most sacred covenants or sacraments that men and women can enter into while in mortality.

These are some of the reasons why the Lord has condemned any sexual relationship outside the bonds of marriage. Happiness can never come from extramarital relationships or acts because participants in immorality "are without God in the world, and they have gone contrary to the nature of God; therefore, they are in a state contrary to the nature of happiness" (Alma 41:11).

Now that we have a better understanding of why morality is so important, we are prepared for a few suggestions on how to withstand sexual pressures.

As you read these few suggestions, I hope you will not dismiss them because they are so simple. I understand most of you will have heard these things all your life. That's the point! We must now learn "not only to say, but to do according to that which I [the Lord] have written" (D&C 84:57).

Our Divine Heritage

The first defense against sexual pressure is to truly believe that we are the sons and daughters of God. We must then try to understand the whys of chastity—that chastity is more than merely avoiding pregnancy or disease but, as Brother Holland explained, is a matter instead of reverencing the *soul* (the spirit and the body), of honoring the *symbol* of total union between a man and a woman, and of recognizing the sacred role of human intimacy as a *sacrament,* or an act that unites us with God (see "Of Souls, Symbols, and Sacraments," pp. 74–85).

Prayer

Then we must involve ourselves in the most basic of religious practices. We must learn to pray—not just learn to say prayers but to truly pray. (We will discuss this in more detail in chapter 6.) "Verily, verily, I say unto you, ye must watch and pray always, lest ye be tempted by the devil, and ye be led away captive by him. . . . Behold, verily, verily, I say unto you, ye must watch and pray always lest ye enter into temptation; for Satan desireth to have you, that he may sift you as wheat." (3 Nephi 18:15, 18.)

Charity

What should we pray for? May I suggest that we learn to pray with all our energy of heart for the gift of charity. I believe there is a direct relationship between charity and chastity. "Charity . . . thinketh no evil, and rejoiceth not in iniquity but rejoiceth in the truth, . . . [and] endureth all things" (Moroni 7:45). Charity is the "pure love of Christ, and it endureth forever" (Moroni 7:47).

But charity is a gift and must be asked for—and not just asked for casually: "Wherefore, my beloved brethren, pray unto the Father with all the energy of heart, that ye may be filled with this love, which he hath bestowed upon all who are true followers of his Son, Jesus Christ; that ye may become the sons of God; that when he shall appear we shall be like him, for we shall see him as he is; that we may have this hope; that we may be purified even as he is pure" (Moroni 7:48). We must pray for purity with "all the energy of heart" in every situation.

When we have prayed for and received this gift of charity (which must happen over and over in our lives), and when we are letting "virtue garnish our thoughts unceasingly," something wonderful happens to us:

> Let thy bowels also be full of charity towards all men, and to the household of faith, and let virtue garnish thy thoughts unceasingly; then shall thy confidence wax strong in the presence of God; and the doctrine of the priesthood shall distil upon thy soul as the dews from heaven.
>
> The Holy Ghost shall be thy constant companion, and thy scepter an unchanging scepter of righteousness and truth; and thy dominion shall be an everlasting dominion and without compulsory means it shall flow unto thee forever and ever. (D&C 121:45–46.)

If we are virtuous, our confidence will be strong, we will have the Holy Ghost, and thus we will see clearly. Then we can resist evil.

Controlling Our Thoughts

When we do not have charity and we lose control of our thoughts, we put ourselves in danger of transgression: "And he that looketh upon a woman to lust after her shall deny the faith, and shall not have the Spirit; and if he repents not he shall be cast out" (D&C 42:23). Lustful thoughts deprive us of the companionship of the Holy Ghost, and without that, our testimonies falter. Then, unable to see things clearly (see Jacob 4:13–14) and blinded by desire, we might surrender to our carnal desires and transgress. If we don't repent, we will be cast out and, as it says in Doctrine and Covenants 63:16, we "shall fear." Rather than have confidence, we will fear! We must pray specifically for charity. Elder Marvin J. Ashton has commented: "Real charity is not something you give away; it is something you acquire and make a part of yourself. And when the virtue of charity becomes implanted in your heart, you are never the same again." (*Ensign,* May 1992, p. 19.)

Avoid Evil

Speaking of young Latter-day Saint men and women, President Spencer W. Kimball has said: "The devil knows how to destroy them. He knows, young men and women, that he cannot tempt you to commit adultery immediately, but he knows too that he can soften you up by lewd associations, vulgar talk, immodest dress, sexy movies, and so on. He knows too that if he can get them to drink or if he can get them into his 'necking, petting' program, the best boys and the best girls will finally succumb and will fall." (*The Miracle of Forgiveness* [Salt Lake City: Bookcraft, 1969], pp. 230–31.) We must avoid situations in which either we have had trouble in the past or we know we could have trouble in the future. We must avoid the pitfalls!

President Kimball has also counseled that we avoid long, lusty, passionate kissing: "Kissing has been prostituted and has been degenerated to develop and express lust instead of affection, honor, and admiration. To kiss in casual dating is asking for trouble. What do kisses mean when given out like pretzels or robbed of sacredness?" (In Sydney Australia Area Conference Report, February 19, 1976, p. 55).

The Church-produced pamphlet *For the Strength of Youth* contains many practical suggestions on how to resist sexual pressures. In one place it deals with modesty in dress and appearance:

> Servants of God have always counseled his children to dress modestly to show respect for him and for themselves. Because the way you dress sends messages about yourself to others and often influences the way you and others act, you should dress in such a way as to bring out the best in yourself and those around you. However, if you wear an immodest bathing suit because it's "the style," it sends a message that you are using your body to get attention and approval, and that modesty is not important (p. 8).

The scriptures contain many examples of those who have succeeded in standing up to the pressures and who were conditioned to "shake at the appearance of sin" (2 Nephi 4:31). If we are to succeed, we need to run from evil and not be afraid of what others may think of us. I realize how difficult that is, but don't we run from things that would destroy us physically? Then why not run from evil that will destroy us spiritually?

Shun Pornography

President Gordon B. Hinckley has given us some wonderful counsel on the subject of pornography:

> You cannot afford in any degree to become involved with pornography, whatever its form. You simply cannot afford to become involved in immoral practices—or to let down the bars of sexual restraint. The emotions that stir within you which make boys attractive to girls and girls attractive to boys are part of a divine plan, but they must be restrained, subdued, and kept under control, or they will destroy you and make you unworthy of many of the great blessings which the Lord has in store for you." (*Ensign,* May 1992, p. 71.)

What greater example could be found of successfully withstanding sexual pressure than Joseph of Egypt? From the days of my youth, his story has inspired me. Joseph is one of my greatest heroes. He knew he was a son of our Heavenly King. He avoided the pitfalls, and when the time came to withstand the pressure, his only concern was to not "sin against God" (Genesis 39:9).

As you know, Joseph had been ripped away from his beloved father, Jacob, and sold by his jealous brothers as a slave into Egypt. Even in slavery the Lord was with Joseph, and the young man prospered. With the Lord's continued blessing, Joseph rose to a position of authority in the household of Potiphar, second only to Potiphar himself. As Joseph carried out his duties in his master's house, Potiphar's wife began to lust after this handsome, strong young Israelite:

> And it came to pass after these things, that his master's wife cast her eyes upon Joseph; and she said, Lie with me.
> But he refused, and said unto his master's wife, Behold, my master wotteth not what is with me in the

house, and he hath committed all that he hath to my hand;

There is none greater in this house than I; neither hath he kept back any thing from me but thee, because thou art his wife: how then can I do this great wickedness, and sin against God?

And it came to pass, as she spake to Joseph day by day, that he hearkened not unto her, to lie by her, or to be with her.

And it came to pass about this time, that Joseph went into the house to do his business; and there was none of the men of the house there within.

And she caught him by his garment, saying, Lie with me: and he left his garment in her hand, and fled, and got him out. (Genesis 39:7–12.)

Joseph ran!

Joseph remembered. He knew he was a son of God. He knew the whys of chastity. He knew why it was not just wrong but also why it was "great wickedness" to express his sexuality outside of marriage. He did not want to disappoint his Father, his Heavenly King.

Oh, that each of us might respond to the sexual pressures in our lives as Joseph did! Then the mists of darkness would begin to fade, and our lights would shine through the darkness of this sin-stained world to bless not only our own lives but also the lives of many of our Father's sons and daughters. We are all born to be kings and queens. We all need help to stay on the well-lighted path that leads to the "tree, whose fruit was desirable to make one happy" (1 Nephi 8:10).

Repentance

There is little doubt that some readers will have struggled and fallen at times or given in to the enormous weight of today's sexual pressures. Please believe that there is hope. You have not gone too far. You can return. Elder Boyd K. Packer has taught us that there is hope:

> In the battle of life, the adversary takes enormous numbers of prisoners, and many who know of no way to escape and are pressed into his service. Every soul confined to a concentration camp of sin and guilt has a key to the gate. The adversary cannot hold them if they know how to use it. The key is labeled *Repentance*. The twin principles of repentance and forgiveness exceed in strength the awesome power of the adversary.
>
> I know of no sins connected with the moral standard for which we cannot be forgiven. I do not exempt abortion. The formula is stated in forty words.
>
> "Behold, he who has repented of his sins, the same is forgiven, and I, the Lord, remember them no more.
>
> "By this ye may know if a man repenteth of his sins— behold, he will confess them and forsake them" (D&C 58:42–43). (*Ensign,* May 1992, p. 68.)

However long and painful the process of repentance, there is hope. There is hope through the atoning sacrifice of Jesus Christ. There is hope that through understanding the whys of chastity and putting into practice the hows, we can withstand the sexual pressures of our modern world. There is hope because as children of our Heavenly King, we were born to be kings and queens.

6

Living the Basics

These modern times require brave sons and brave daughters of God. They require that we come to Christ and the Father by obtaining and maintaining the guidance of the Holy Spirit. In obtaining that Spirit we must incorporate some simple, basic principles into our daily lives. These basics give us life, light, and spiritual self-confidence. They are service, scriptures, prayer, and prophets. Sometimes we hear about them so much we forget the power of their simplicity. President Marion G. Romney taught:

> As conditions worsen, it becomes more apparent every day that we are on a collision course with disaster. I am persuaded that nothing short of the guidance of the Holy Spirit can bring us through safely. I call attention to our unpleasant situation not because I want you to be discouraged, but because I want you to see and clearly recognize the predicament of the world in which we live. . . .

If you want to obtain and keep the guidance of the Spirit, you can do so by following this simple four-point program.

One, pray. Pray diligently. Pray with each other. Pray in public in the proper places, but never forget the counsel of the Savior:

"When thou prayest, enter into thy closet, and when thou hast shut thy door, pray to thy Father which is in secret: and thy Father which seeth in secret shall reward thee openly" (Matt. 6:6).

Learn to talk to the Lord; call upon his name in great faith and confidence.

Second, study and learn the gospel.

Third, live righteously; repent of your sins by confessing them and forsaking them. Then conform to the teachings of the gospel.

Fourth, give service in the Church.

If you will do these things, you will get the guidance of the Holy Spirit and you will go through this world successfully, regardless of what the people of the world say or do. (*Ensign,* January 1980, pp. 2, 5.)

Service, scriptures, prayers, and prophets—the simple four-step program to obtain and keep the guidance of the Spirit. These basics are the pathway to the Savior. Incorporating them into our daily lives not only helps us to be brave but also allows us to see clearly, to see things as "they really are" and "as they really will be" (see Jacob 4:13). They help us to stay focused, which helps us to stay moral and righteous, which helps us to stay free, which allows us to "dream dreams" and "see visions." This formula has been the foundation for all who have remained spiritually strong.

In chapter 2 we briefly mentioned that the converted Lamanites stayed strong because they followed these basic principles (see Helaman 15:7–8). We also discussed that the ancients did not dwindle in unbelief, because they had the scriptures "always before [their] eyes" (see Mosiah 1:5).

Before we discuss each of these simple steps, we must discuss where they lead us. Our goal is to come to Christ and our Father. President Thomas S. Monson explains that before we can successfully undertake a personal search for Jesus Christ, we must first make room for him in our hearts. Service, scriptures, prayers, and prophets become the daily stepping-stones for making room for Christ in our lives.

> In these busy days there are many who have time for golf, time for shopping, time for work, time for play—but no time for Christ.
>
> Lovely homes dot the land and provide rooms for eating, rooms for sleeping, playrooms, sewing rooms, television rooms, but no room for Christ.
>
> Do we get a pang of conscience as we recall his own words: "The foxes have holes, and birds of the air have nests; but the Son of man hath not where to lay his head." (Matt. 8:20.) Or do we flush with embarrassment when we remember, "And she brought forth her firstborn son, and wrapped him in swaddling clothes, and laid him in a manger; because there was no room for them in the inn." (Luke 2:7.) No room. No room. No room. Ever has it been. . . .
>
> . . . This is the Jesus whom we seek. This is our brother whom we love. This is Christ the Lord, whom we serve. I testify that he lives, for I speak as one who has found him. (*Ensign*, December 1990, pp. 4–5.)

We must progress to a point in our understanding and appreciation of Christ's atonement where we realize that this most supreme of all events in the universe is broader and covers more than cleansing us of our sins.

Being cleansed from our sins is critical to lift us from our fallen state. But the Atonement is far more vast and encompasses overcoming everything that would keep us from being at one with God. Alma writes:

> For behold, I say unto you there be many things to come; and behold, there is one thing which is of more importance than they all—for behold, the time is not far distant that the Redeemer liveth and cometh among his people. . . .
>
> And he shall go forth, suffering pains and afflictions and temptations of every kind; and this that the word might be fulfilled which saith he will take upon him the pains and the sicknesses of his people.
>
> And he will take upon him death, that he may loose the bands of death which bind his people; and he will take upon him their infirmities, that his bowels may be filled with mercy, according to the flesh, that he may know according to the flesh how to succor his people according to their infirmities.
>
> Now the Spirit knoweth all things; nevertheless the Son of God suffereth according to the flesh that he might take upon him the sins of his people, that he might blot out their transgressions according to the power of his deliverance; and now behold, this is the testimony which is in me. (Alma 7:7, 11–13.)

He takes upon himself our pains, our sicknesses, our infirmities, our sins, and that monster, death. May I add to Alma's thoughts that he even takes upon himself our sorrows, our griefs, our discouragements, and our depressions—anything that would keep us from him. Is this why the Master tenderly speaks to all: "Come back. Come up. Come in. Come home. Come unto me." (Thomas S. Monson, *Ensign,* June 1993, p. 2.) Can you and I accept this divine invitation to exaltation? What are we waiting for? Why not make the commitment now? Today?

If you have been away from the Church for any reason, please come back. The Lord and the Saints need you. And you need them. If you have been depressed, discouraged, or distraught, please come up. Arise from the dust and be men and women of Christ. (See 2 Nephi 1:21 and Helaman 3:29.)

If you're not sure the gospel or the Church is for you, please come in. Don't feel lonely or embarrassed. Please don't stand outside looking in. Walk through the door.

If you have been a prodigal, if you have broken your covenants or have never made them, please come home. The fire is warm; the doors are open. We love you. Elder Boyd K. Packer has said: "Say the word *temple.* Say it quietly and reverently. Say it over and over again. *Temple. Temple. Temple.* Add the word *holy. Holy Temple.* Say it as though it were capitalized, no matter where it appears in the sentence.

"Temple. One other word is equal in importance to a Latter-day Saint. *Home.* Put the words *holy temple* and *home* together, and you have described the house of the Lord!" (*Ensign,* May 1993, pp. 20–21.) The temple is home. Please come home.

Do you feel you are a failure? Have you lost all hope? Do you feel that life is not worth living? Please, the Master invites, "Come unto me." Let him be the Gentle Healer. Has he not tenderly asked: "Will ye not now return unto me, and repent of your sins, and be converted, that I may heal you?" (3 Nephi 9:13.) We must somehow with our service, our scriptures, our prayers, and our prophets allow the Savior to place his hands upon us and our families so that we might live.

In Mark 5 is a touching story of the healing of Jairus's daughter. As Jairus encountered Christ, he fell at his feet and "besought him greatly, saying, My little daughter lieth at the point of death: I pray thee, come and lay thy hands on her, that she may be healed; and she shall live" (see Mark 5:23).

Elder Howard W. Hunter commented on this verse of scripture. "These are not only the words of faith of a father torn with grief but are also a reminder to us that whatever Jesus lays his hands upon lives. If Jesus lays his hands upon a marriage, it lives. If he is allowed to lay his hands on a family, it lives." (*Ensign*, November 1979, p. 65.)

We can live if we will allow the Savior to lay his hands upon us. Our families, our relationships, everything can live with his touch. Can we allow him to do so by bringing service, scriptures, prayers, and prophets into our daily lives and families?

Of course, this simple, basic, four-point program will not keep heartache and tragedy from coming into our lives, but it might help us to be free from bitterness, anger, sorrow, and pain. Often when tragedy comes into our lives it has nothing to do with anything we have done. For example, Elder Boyd K. Packer has taught us about the measure of a successful parent:

It is a great challenge to raise a family in the darkening mists of our moral environment.

We emphasize that the greatest work you will do will be within the walls of your home (see Harold B. Lee, *Ensign*, July 1973, p. 98), and that "no other success can compensate for failure in the home" (David O. McKay, *Improvement Era*, June 1964, p. 445).

The measure of our success as parents, however, will not rest solely on how our children turn out. That judgment would be just only if we could raise our families in a perfectly moral environment, and that now is not possible.

It is not uncommon for responsible parents to lose one of their children, for a time, to influences over which they have no control. They agonize over rebellious sons or daughters. They are puzzled over why they are so helpless when they have tried so hard to do what they should.

It is my conviction that those wicked influences one day will be overruled.

"The Prophet Joseph Smith declared—and he never taught a more comforting doctrine—that the eternal sealings of faithful parents and the divine promises made to them for valiant service in the Cause of Truth, would save not only themselves, but likewise their posterity. Though some of the sheep may wander, the eye of the Shepherd is upon them, and sooner or later they will feel the tentacles of Divine Providence reaching out after them and drawing them back to the fold. Either in this life or the life to come, they will return. They will have to pay their debt to justice; they will suffer for their sins; and may tread a thorny path; but if it leads them at last, like the penitent Prodigal, to a loving and forgiving father's heart and home, the painful experience will not have been in vain. Pray for your careless and disobedient children; hold on to them with your faith. Hope on, trust on, till you see the salvation of God." (Orson F. Whitney, in Conference Report, Apr. 1929, p. 110.)

We cannot overemphasize the value of temple marriage, the binding ties of the sealing ordinance, and the standards of worthiness required of them. When parents keep the covenants they have made at the altar of the temple, their children will be forever bound to them. President Brigham Young said:

"Let the father and mother, who are members of this Church and Kingdom, take a righteous course, and strive with all their might never to do a wrong, but to do good all their lives; if they have one child or one hundred children, if they conduct themselves towards them as they should, binding them to the Lord by their faith and prayers, I care not where those children go, they are bound up to their parents by an everlasting tie, and no power of earth or hell can separate them from their parents in eternity; they will return again to the fountain from whence they sprang." (*Doctrines of Salvation,* comp. Bruce R. McConkie, 3 vols., Joseph Fielding Smith, 2:90–91.) (*Ensign,* May 1992, p. 68.)

The Atonement both allows and enables people to change. It permits us to take advantage of "the great plan of happiness" (Alma 42:8).

Let us now discuss the four simple steps for receiving the guidance of the Holy Spirit.

1. *Service in the Church.* Service in the Church takes on a whole new meaning when we understand the difference between the Lord's Church and man-made institutions.

In order to want to serve diligently in the Church without complaint or feeling overburdened, a knowledge of whose work this really is is critical. This is not just another therapeutic belief system to help men and women cope with everyday trials and problems. It is not a church of men—nor of man—organized to promote private or political agendas. It is the Church of God, the true Church of Jesus Christ. It is not run nor can it be run like other earthly organizations. "The Church of Jesus Christ of Latter-day Saints, however, is neither a democracy nor a republic. His is a kingdom—the kingdom of God on earth. His is a hierarchal church, with ultimate authority at the top. The Lord directs his anointed servants. They testify to all the world that God has again spoken. The heavens have been opened. A living linkage has been formed between heaven and earth in our day." (Russell M. Nelson, *Ensign,* May 1993, p. 38.)

Elder M. Russell Ballard expounds: "The scriptures state clearly that while our respective callings may be different and may change from time to time, all callings are important to the operation of the Church. . . . This is not man's work nor woman's work; it is *all* God's work, which is centered on the atonement of our Lord Jesus Christ. . . .

". . . Priesthood is for service, not servitude; compassion, not compulsion; caring, not control. Those who think otherwise are operating outside the parameters of priesthood authority." (*Ensign*, November 1993, pp. 77–78.)

Any service to Christ and our Father is high honor. The old cliché of "It's not where but how we serve" is true. Every position, every calling, is significant in this kingdom.

Assigned to each individual who bears the priesthood or who serves in any capacity in the Church is a loving priesthood leader. This is because "mine house is a house of order, saith the Lord God, and not a house of confusion" (D&C 132:8). Elder Russell M. Nelson commented on this order and suggested some do's and don'ts for each person who receives a call to serve in the Church:

> That order also defines bounds of revelation. The Prophet Joseph Smith taught that "it is contrary to the economy of God for any member of the Church, or any one, to receive instruction for those in authority, higher than themselves." (*Teachings of the Prophet Joseph Smith*, p. 21.) That same principle precludes receiving revelation for anyone outside one's defined circle of responsibility.
>
> Honoring the priesthood also means to honor your personal call to serve. A few do's and don'ts may be helpful:
>
> • Do learn to take counsel. Seek direction from file leaders and receive it willingly.
>
> • Don't speak ill of Church leaders.
>
> • Don't covet a calling or position.
>
> • Don't second-guess who should or should not have been called.
>
> • Don't refuse an opportunity to serve.
>
> • Don't resign from a call. Do inform leaders of changing circumstances in your life, knowing that leaders will weigh all factors when prayerfully considering the proper timing of your release." (*Ensign*, May 1993, p. 39.)

The Savior, through the Prophet Joseph Smith, taught each of us how to approach whatever calling we have in the kingdom: "Wherefore, now let every man learn his duty, and to act in the office in which he is appointed, in all diligence. He that is slothful shall not be counted worthy to stand, and he that learns not his duty and shows himself not approved shall not be counted worthy to stand. Even so. Amen." (D&C 107:99–100.)

We must never forget the prophetic words of President Thomas S. Monson, "Whom the Lord calls, the Lord qualifies" (as quoted in Neil L. Anderson, *Ensign,* May 1993, p. 82). He will qualify us! This is his work!

"God does not begin by asking us about our ability, but only about our availability, and if we then prove our dependability, he will increase our capability!" (Neal A. Maxwell, *Ensign,* July 1975, p. 7.)

2. *Scriptures.* Several years ago while teaching seminary, I had some students who thought it was funny to give me a hard time. They would chant the theme of a Lego TV commercial, but change the words hoping to irritate me. They would chant: "Jack, Jack, he's a scripture maniac." Of course, it was supposed to say, "Jack, Jack, he's a Lego maniac." It had just the opposite effect from what they jokingly wanted. After kindly asking them not to refer to me as Jack, I thanked them for the compliment. They had no idea that complaining of receiving too much scripture in class was a great compliment!

I love the holy scriptures! They are a treasure. Searching them is like taking a long, hot shower. I love to stay in the shower and let the hot, steaming water drench my entire body. When we allow the living waters of the scriptures to drench us daily, our love for them becomes delicious (see Alma 32:28). Joseph Smith stated, "He who reads it oftenest will like it best" (*Teachings of the Prophet Joseph Smith,* p. 56).

The psalmist wrote, "How sweet are thy words unto my taste! yea, sweeter than honey to my mouth! . . . Thy word is a lamp unto my feet, and a light unto my path." (Psalm 119:103, 105.)

Have the scriptures become sweet to our taste and like honey to our mouths? Do they guide our decision-making process? President Harold B. Lee taught:

> I say that we need to teach our people to find their answers in the scriptures. If only each of us would be wise enough to say that we aren't able to answer any question unless we can find a doctrinal answer in the scriptures! And if we hear someone teaching something that is contrary to what is in the scriptures, each of us may know whether the things spoken are false—it is as simple as that. But the unfortunate thing is that so many of us are not reading the scriptures. We do not know what is in them, therefore we speculate about the things that we ought to have found in the scriptures themselves. I think that therein is one of our biggest dangers of today. (*Ensign*, December 1972, p. 3.)

There is a power that comes from the scriptures that can come in no other way. In fact, it is my opinion that other than being immersed in prayer, drenching ourselves daily in the living waters of the scriptures is the greatest way to not only be brave but also to continue in our bravery and courage. However, it takes work and effort to unlock the scriptures' beauty, wisdom, and knowledge. Elder Boyd K. Packer has said: "For His own reasons, the Lord provides answers to some questions, with pieces placed here and there throughout the scriptures. We are to find them; we are to *earn* them. In that way sacred things are hidden from the insincere." (*Ensign*, November 1983, p. 17.)

What Nephi and Alma taught is true: "Angels speak by the power of the Holy Ghost; wherefore, they speak the words of Christ. Wherefore, I said unto you, feast upon the words of Christ; for behold, the words of Christ will tell you all things what ye should do." (2 Nephi 32:3.)

"And now, as the preaching of the word had a great tendency to lead the people to do that which was just— yea, it had had more powerful effect upon the minds of the people than the sword, or anything else, which had happened unto them—therefore Alma thought it was ex- pedient that they should try the virtue of the word of God" (Alma 31:5).

Consider these words:

> If your students [referring to seminary and institute stu- dents] are acquainted with the revelations, there is no question—personal or social or political or occupational— that need go unanswered. Therein is contained the fulness of the everlasting gospel. Therein we find principles of truth that will resolve every confusion and every problem and every dilemma that will face the human family or any individual in it. (Boyd K. Packer, "Teach the Scriptures," Address to Religious Educators, October 14, 1977, p. 5.)

> I think that people who study the scriptures get a di- mension to their life that nobody else gets and that can't be gained in any way except by studying the scriptures. There's an increase in faith and a desire to do what's right and a feeling of inspiration and understanding that comes to people who study the gospel—meaning particularly the standard works—and who ponder the principles, that can't come in any other way. (Bruce R. McConkie, *Church News*, January 24, 1976, p. 4.)

Our beloved Prophet Joseph Smith commented on how our individual testimonies can be strengthened by studying the scriptures:

> Search the scriptures—search the revelations which we publish, and ask your Heavenly Father, in the name of His

Son Jesus Christ, to manifest the truth unto you, and if you do it with an eye single to His glory nothing doubting, He will answer you by the power of His Holy Spirit. You will then know for yourselves and not for another. You will not then be dependent on man for the knowledge of God; nor will there be any room for speculation. No; for when men receive their instruction from Him that made them, they know how He will save them. Then again we say; Search the Scriptures, search the Prophets and learn what portion of them belongs to you. (*Teachings of the Prophet Joseph Smith,* pp. 11–12.)

3. *Prayer.* So much has been written about prayer, and it is talked about at such great length, that it may seem a little laborious to address the issue again. However, is discussing breathing in connection with life laborious? Just as breathing is the most basic fundamental of life, so prayer is the most basic fundamental to obtaining and maintaining the Spirit. "Prayer is the simplest form of speech / That infant lips can try" ("Prayer Is the Soul's Sincere Desire," *Hymns,* no. 145).

Twelve times in the Doctrine and Covenants the Lord instructs us to "pray always" so that we might obtain his various blessings. He instructs us to "pray always" in order to conquer Satan (see D&C 19:38), to avoid temptation (see D&C 20:33; 31:12), to understand the scriptures (see D&C 32:4), to be ready for the Second Coming (see D&C 33:17), to avoid temptation and abide the Second Coming (see D&C 61:39), to faint not (see D&C 75:11), to endure to the Second Coming (see D&C 88:126), to ensure that all things will work for our good (see D&C 90:24), and to prevent Satan from overcoming us (see D&C 93:49).

Can we begin to get the message? These are only a few verses from but one volume of scripture. The scriptures are filled with admonitions to pray. Pray. Pray. Pray.

We can overcome personal weaknesses and bad habits. Even degrading habits. We can win the personal battles being waged within each of us. If we will but pray, and not just say prayers, the Lord will help us through any difficulty. One of the most comforting scriptures in all of holy writ is in Doctrine and Covenants 104:82, wherein the Lord instructs, "And inasmuch as ye are humble and faithful and call upon my name, behold, I will give you the victory."

He will give us the victory. But we must be humble and we must pray. So often, as mentioned above, we are good at saying prayers but not so good at praying. Sometimes we are so caught up in repeating familiar phrases and using "vain repetitions" that we forget to really talk to our Father. Perhaps the sharing of a little story can illustrate this point.

Two young brothers were arrested one Saturday night for vandalizing an old vacant home. The arresting officer knew they were not bad boys but wanted to scare them a little in hopes that he might teach them a valuable lesson in their young lives. He took them to jail in handcuffs, booked them, and fingerprinted them. After this rough treatment, the boys were terrified and had vowed in their hearts never to do anything wrong again.

The officer was quite pleased with his teaching. When he felt that he had taught the lesson well enough, he phoned the boys' father, explained everything, and asked him to come and pick up the boys. Their father responded with a question: "Can you legally keep them in jail for twenty-four hours?"

"Well, sure," responded the officer. "But they've learned their lesson and are ready to go home now."

The father interjected, "If you can keep them in jail for twenty-four hours, I would like you to do so."

"But, sir. You don't understand. I've already scared

them to death, and I'm sure you won't have a problem with them in the future."

Emphatically the father insisted: "If you can legally keep them, I want them to stay!"

"Sir?" the officer asked. "Aren't you a Mormon?"

"Yes," was the reply.

"Don't you want your boys in church tomorrow morning?"

"No! I want them in jail so they can really learn a lesson."

The officer couldn't believe it, and neither could the two brothers.

The next morning when the officer took them breakfast, he stopped and listened as they discussed their dad having left them in jail all night long.

"I can't believe it!" the oldest boy muttered. "He left us all night!"

"Yeah," responded the younger of the two. "I've never felt bad about missing church until someone told me I couldn't go."

Looking at his watch, the oldest said, "We've already missed priesthood meeting, and Sunday School will start in five minutes."

The younger brother then came up with a grand idea: "Why don't we have our own Sunday School. I'll pray if you'll give us a lesson."

The older brother agreed. The officer continued to watch and listen, still holding their plates of food. Then the younger brother began to pray the only way he knew how: "Dear Heavenly Father. We're so grateful that we could all be here today. We're grateful for this beautiful building we have to meet in." And then the kicker. "Please bless all those that aren't with us this week, that they will be with us next week!"

Have we become like the young man in the preceding

story? Are we so busy saying prayers that we don't really pray? Saying prayers is much much different than praying to our holy Heavenly Father.

President Marion G. Romney was a man who knew how to pray. In fact, at President Romney's funeral, President Benson, President Hinckley, and Elder Packer all commented on his ability to pray.

President Ezra Taft Benson said of him, "You have never heard a man pray until you have heard President Romney pray. Many men say prayers, but few talk to the Lord. President Romney was one who knew how. None of his Brethren had any question about his nearness to the Lord. His prayers were so earnest and his appeals so sincere, none could doubt that the Lord was near to him. President Kimball once said of him, 'All is holy where this man kneels.'" (*Ensign,* July 1988, p. 76.)

Can anyone think of a greater compliment than to have a prophet feel that "all is holy where this man kneels?"

President Gordon B. Hinckley commented:

I loved him for his prayers. I have never heard any man pray quite as Marion G. Romney prayed. So many of our prayers are like one-way telephone conversations in which we ring a number, place an order, and then hang up. Brother Romney's prayers were simple, yet wonderfully profound. Whenever he prayed it seemed to me that he did so as he must have done when he was a small, innocent boy in Mexico. There was no element of sophistication. There was no guile. There was no pretense. There was little in the way of lofty language or elaborate phrasing. Rather, there was conversation. He spoke with God his Eternal Father as if he were facing a friend, talking with him in a conversation, expressing his feelings and his needs. (*Ensign,* July 1988, p. 76.)

Can we comprehend what President Hinckley was saying? President Hinckley has heard some very spiritual men talk to God, but no one prayed quite as President Romney prayed.

Elder Boyd K. Packer felt very similar:

> Of all the lessons I've learned from this man and that we have learned—my brethren of the Twelve and we of the Church—the [greatest] lesson was centered in the subject of revelation. From him we saw by demonstration the difference between praying and simply saying prayers. Of all the men I have known, no one was more sure than Brother Romney of the process of divine revelation. If you read his sermons carefully, you will find hidden there such phrases as "I know that voice when He speaks," and in his conversations and his talks to more intimate groups, his testimony was firm and certain and unshaken. (*Ensign,* July 1988, p. 78.)

The reason for quoting these three prophets and Apostles is that all of us could learn from President Romney. He taught:

> If we are to be on the side of truth, we must have the Spirit of the Lord. To the obtaining of that Spirit, prayer is an indispensable prerequisite. Praying will keep one's vision clear on this question of loyalty as on all other questions. By praying I do not mean, however, just saying prayers. Prayers may be said in a perfunctory manner. Access to the Spirit of God, which is a directing power, cannot be so obtained. The divine injunction to pray is not to be satisfied in a casual manner nor by an effort to obtain divine approval of a predetermined course. A firm resolve to comply with the will of God must accompany the petition for knowledge as to what His will is. When one brings himself to the position that he will pursue the truth wherever it

may lead, even though it may require a reversal of his former position, he can, without hypocrisy, go before the Lord in prayer. Then, when he prays with all the energy of his soul, he is entitled to and he will receive guidance. The mind and will of the Lord as to the course he should take will be made known to him.

I assure you, however, that the Spirit of the Lord will never direct a person to take a position in opposition to the counsel of the Presidency of His Church. (Conference Report, April 1942, p. 19.)

When we truly pray by the power of the Spirit, we may pray with confidence, knowing that the Spirit of the Lord will never direct us contrary to the current position of the First Presidency.

With such clear direction, why do so many continue to struggle with making the effort to call upon God daily with full purpose of heart? Perhaps a poem can emphasize this point. The poem was written by a former member of the Church shortly before he was to be executed for murder.

The Wrong Path Chosen

I wonder where I went wrong,
In my youth and in my past.
Life's changes were quite sudden
To bring good to bad so fast.

In eagerness I started out
Life's mysteries to explore.
My parents gave me a good life.
In foolishness I sought more.

My youth held some accomplishments
Great was my hope to please.
My desires to serve the Lord
Brought me often to my knees.

Upon my path temptations came
Which alone, I couldn't escape.
Too proud to call for needed help
I chose my dreadful fate.

My future now holds little hope
And my life is full of fear.
The sentence of death upon me
Calls hell's presence oh so near.

Deep within these prison walls
I'll spend the rest of life.
No more dreams or hopes or pleasures.
Never to have my own family or wife.

The nights are getting longer,
The days . . . yet longer still.
I need to find some inner strength
To climb my last big hill.

I pray it's not too late for me
To purge my soul from sin,
Or remove the doubt within my heart
So heaven may let me in.

To young people I would say,
Be true! Be just! Be fair!
Follow the teachings of the Lord,
And fill your days with prayer.

Both men, the prophet and the murderer, learned the same lesson, although to very different degrees. Prayer and fasting bring us close to the Lord. One learned by coming unto God and the other from falling away from God. One died with peace, knowing his Father in Heaven was pleased with his sojourn in mortality. The other died knowing he had drifted away and had disappointed not only Father in Heaven but also himself, his family, his friends, and the families of his victims. What joy comes to the heart of him who prays! What sorrow fills the breast of him who ceases to pray! May we all pray always so that each of us "may come off conqueror; . . . that [we] may escape the hands of the servants of Satan that do uphold his work" (D&C 10:5).

4. *Prophets.* Elder Neal A. Maxwell made a profound statement in 1979 to a group of religious educators. He said: "Now we are entering times wherein there will be for all of us as Church members, in my judgment, some special challenges which will require of us that we follow the Brethren. All the easy things that the Church has had to do have been done. From now on, it's high adventure, and followership is going to be tested in some interesting ways." ("The Old Testament: Relevancy Within Antiquity," *The Third Annual Church Educational System Religious Educators' Symposium* [Salt Lake City: The Church of Jesus Christ of Latter-day Saints, 1979], p. 12.)

What a time to be alive! A time of high adventure. A time of courage. A time of visions and dreams. A time of freedom. A time of followership.

Can we be followers as well as leaders? The Savior told the Prophet Joseph Smith that following the prophet would keep the gates of Hell shut against us:

> Wherefore, meaning the church, thou shalt give heed unto all his words and commandments which he shall give unto you as he receiveth them, walking in all holiness before me;
>
> For his word ye shall receive, as if from mine own mouth, in all patience and faith.
>
> For by doing these things the gates of hell shall not prevail against you; yea, and the Lord God will disperse the powers of darkness from before you, and cause the heavens to shake for your good, and his name's glory.
>
> For thus saith the Lord God: Him have I inspired to

move the cause of Zion in mighty power for good, and his diligence I know, and his prayers I have heard. (D&C 21:4–7.)

He also said that those who wouldn't listen to the Apostles and prophets would be cut off from among the people (see D&C 1:14). The Lord speaks through Apostles and prophets (see D&C 43). It has always been so. We must have the courage to follow. Spirituality is maintained from following the Lord's anointed. It is one of the four simple basic steps to getting and maintaining the Holy Ghost.

Are they not worthy of our loyalty? Are not their teachings and fruits worthy of our trust and commitment? Have not most of them, through the years, proven to be brave sons of our Father? Indeed, they have been brave to the very end.

Many of the Church's Presidents have become physically incapacitated as advancing years have come upon them. This list has included Presidents Kimball and Benson. Rather than being critical of them, we should learn from their bravery and fortitude. Perhaps the greatest lesson we can learn from this is that even prophets must be brave and endure to the end! Besides, as President Gordon B. Hinckley has taught, the Lord has a backup system:

Some people, evidently not knowing the system, worry that because of the President's age, the Church faces a crisis. They seem not to realize that there is a backup system. In the very nature of this system there is always on board a trained crew, if I may so speak of them. They have been thoroughly schooled in Church procedures. More importantly, they also hold the keys of the eternal priesthood of God. They, too, have been put in place by the Lord." (*Ensign*, November 1992, p. 53.)

The Lord is in charge! This is the church and kingdom of Jesus Christ! He is at the helm. He it is who set up a system that could handle or deal with the failing health or absence of a member of the First Presidency. Following prophets is a virtue, not a weakness.

The bravery of President Howard W. Hunter is remarkable. After surgery, while standing at the pulpit in general conference, his legs locked; in an instant, all who watched saw the President of the Quorum of the Twelve fall backwards into a potted plant. President Monson and Elder Packer immediately leapt up and rushed to his aid. As they raised him from the floor, still standing on stiff legs, his eyes caught the words of his talk on the teleprompter, and he never missed a beat! President Hunter's talk went on as planned, with President Monson standing at his side. What dignity! What majesty! What bravery! How many of us, after falling down in front of the entire Church, would have had the courage to keep going?

Years later, still in fragile health, this dear Apostle of the Lord was just commencing a talk at BYU's Marriott Center when a man walked up to him with something in his hand that he said was a detonator and ordered President Hunter to read a message he had prepared. With no knowledge that the detonator was actually just a telephone receiver wrapped in tape, President Hunter simply refused. What courage! What peace in knowing the plan! After the man was apprehended and President Hunter was checked over by a physician, he calmly walked to the microphone and began, "I want to tell you how good your voices sound," referring to the congregation's earlier spontaneous singing of the hymn, "We Thank Thee, O God, for a Prophet." He then began his planned address: "Life has a fair number of challenges in it, and that's true of life in the 1990s." (See "Suspect

Linked to Guns Left at Square," Deseret News, February 8, 1993, p. A-1.)

He talked as a prophet, as if nothing had happened that February 1993 evening. Brethren and sisters, we are not led by cowards or weaklings. We are led by Apostles and prophets of Jesus Christ! We must follow them or lose the Spirit. "And the arm of the Lord shall be revealed; and the day cometh that they who will not hear the voice of the Lord, neither the voice of his servants, neither give heed to the words of the prophets and apostles, shall be cut off from among the people" (D&C 1:14).

Have there ever been greater examples of bravery than our beloved prophet Joseph Smith and our Savior Jesus Christ?

As the Prophet crossed the Mississippi River in hopes of escaping from his enemies, a letter was brought to him from his wife, Emma. Those who brought the letter accused Joseph of being cowardly and of leaving "the flock to the wolves." After all Joseph had been through, some had the gall to accuse him of cowardice. After this seething comment, he sadly uttered, "If my life is of no value to my friends it is of none to myself." (See *History of the Church,* 6:549).

He then crossed the river and headed for Carthage. The following statement describes Joseph's feelings as he left his home for the last time:

> When Joseph went to Carthage to deliver himself up to the pretended requirements of the law, two or three days previous to his assassination, he said: "I am going like a lamb to the slaughter; but I am calm as a summer's morning; I have a conscience void of offense towards God, and towards all men. I shall die innocent, and it shall yet be said of me—he was murdered in cold blood." (D&C 135:4).

Joseph knew it was the end for him, but still he went.

President John Taylor wrote of the event:

> To seal the testimony of this book and the Book of
> Mormon, we announce the martyrdom of Joseph Smith
> the Prophet, and Hyrum Smith the Patriarch. They were
> shot in Carthage jail, on the 27th of June, 1844, about five
> o'clock p.m., by an armed mob—painted black—of from
> 150 to 200 persons. Hyrum was shot first and fell calmly,
> exclaiming: *I am a dead man!* Joseph leaped from the win-
> dow, and was shot dead in the attempt, exclaiming: *O Lord
> my God!* They were both shot after they were dead, in a
> brutal manner, and both received four balls. (D&C 135:1.)

Joseph was anything but a coward! He and his
brother Hyrum died as brave sons of God.

The Savior showed us all the way to be brave and his
ability to follow the One placed over him in authority.
Luke records:

> And he was withdrawn from them about a stone's cast,
> and kneeled down, and prayed,
> Saying, Father, if thou be willing, remove this cup from
> me: nevertheless not my will, but thine, be done.
> And there appeared an angel unto him from heaven,
> strengthening him.
> And being in an agony he prayed more earnestly: and
> his sweat was as it were great drops of blood falling down
> to the ground. (Luke 22:41–44.)

He was brave enough to give away his will in order to
succumb to the will of his Father. What bravery! What
courage! What love! Can we not do the same? Can we
have the courage, in all situations, through all trials and
temptations, to say, "Not my will be done, but thine"?
The will of the Lord is given to us today through his
anointed Apostles and prophets. He himself has de-

clared, "And this is the ensample unto them, that they shall speak as they are moved upon by the Holy Ghost. And whatsoever they shall speak when moved upon by the Holy Ghost shall be scripture, shall be the will of the Lord, shall be the mind of the Lord, shall be the word of the Lord, shall be the voice of the Lord, and the power of God unto salvation." (D&C 68:3–4.)

May we have the bravery and courage to "come, listen to a prophet's voice, and hear the word of God" (*Hymns,* no. 21).

7

Why We Need the
Book of Mormon

Dreaming dreams, seeing visions, maintaining freedom, being brave, living the basics—if we're not careful, it could all seem overwhelming. Our roots must grow deep and take hold (see Alma 32). Our foundation must be a "sure foundation." Then, with a secure root system and a sure foundation, when the storms of life descend, as they do in all our lives, and as "the devil shall send forth his mighty winds, yea, his shafts in the whirlwind, yea, when all his hail and his mighty storm shall beat upon [us]," we will not fall and will not be withered with the heat of the day (see Helaman 5:12; see also Matthew 13:1–9). The sure foundation is, of course, Christ, our Savior and our Redeemer. He is not only the rock upon which we must build, but he is "the way, the truth, and the life" (John 14:6). He is the light and the life of the world (see John 8:12). He is the Messiah, the "Holy One of Israel" (2 Nephi 9:41).

What happens to us as we grow older? Why does the innocence of our childhood leave us? Why do we so often become hardened to the finer sensitivities of the Spirit? As we mature, shouldn't we increase in faith and righteousness rather than decrease? In our childlike innocence we are meek. We love Jesus and we love to hear stories about him. What happens to that faith? Do we, in our intelligence and wisdom, lose sight of why we need him so desperately? Or is it that disappointment and reality slaps us so hard in the face that we question not only our need for him but also his very existence? If he exists, and if his gospel is one of gladness, happiness, and joy, why is there so much suffering, pain, and sorrow in the world around us?

The answers to these very questions are the essence of why we need Christ. Let me illustrate. Many years ago when our oldest children were small, I took the opportunity to tuck our second daughter into bed. I then lay down next to her. She asked me to tell her many stories. Her eight-year-old mind was intensely inquisitive. She asked me if I would turn on the light and read her a story from the *Friend*. As we thumbed through the magazine together, she noticed a picture of Nephi standing over Laban's drunken body with his sword raised to cut off Laban's head. She let out a cry: "Daddy! Read that one. I love this story."

I remember thinking how strange it seemed for an eight-year-old girl to be excited about Nephi cutting off Laban's head. Nevertheless, I read the story. When I finished, there was a long pause. You could almost see a film going on in her head. She looked at me as if she were embarrassed. She said, "Dad, I really like this story out of the *Friend,* but I like it a lot better out of the Book of Mormon."

I didn't quite know how to respond. After holding

her in my arms and secretly praying that she would feel that way when she was a teenager, I asked her why she felt the way she did. All she mentioned was that it felt different when it was read from the Book of Mormon. Though she didn't understand everything when we read from the scriptures, in her innocence and childlike faith she could feel the Spirit. She knew that the Lord had commanded Nephi to slay Laban; therefore, it was okay to do it. Her faith was sweet and profoundly simple.

Since then I have thought often of Parley P. Pratt's experience with reading the Book of Mormon for the first time. He wrote:

> I read all day; eating was a burden, I had no desire for food; sleep was a burden when the night came, for I preferred reading to sleep.
>
> As I read, the spirit of the Lord was upon me, and I knew and comprehended that the book was true, as plainly and manifestly as a man comprehends and knows that he exists. My joy was now full, as it were, and I rejoiced sufficiently to more than pay me for all the sorrows, sacrifices and toils of my life. I soon determined to see the young man who had been the instrument of its discovery and translation." (*Autobiography of Parley P. Pratt* [Salt Lake City: Deseret Book Co., 1938], p. 37.)

Perhaps our problem as we grow older is that we try to think so much in our approach to spiritual things that we become "past feeling" (see 1 Nephi 17:45). We then begin to rely on ourselves and forget why we need Christ. President Benson has taught, "Just as a man does not really desire food until he is hungry, so he does not desire the salvation of Christ until he knows why he needs Christ.

"No one adequately and properly knows why he needs Christ until he understands and accepts the doctrine of the Fall and its effect upon all mankind. And no other book in the world explains this vital doctrine nearly as well as the Book of Mormon." (*Ensign,* May 1987, p. 85.)

One major reason for being in the Book of Mormon daily is so we can know why we need Christ! As we know why we need him, we will desire to follow him and be even as he is (see 3 Nephi 27:27). The Prophet Joseph Smith taught, "I told the brethren that the Book of Mormon was the most correct of any book on earth, and the keystone of our religion, and a man would get nearer to God by abiding by its precepts, than by any other book" (*History of the Church,* 4:461).

The title page of the book testifies that one of the book's major purposes is "to the convincing of the Jew and Gentile that Jesus is the Christ, the Eternal God, manifesting himself unto all nations."

As we discussed in chapter 4, there is a power that comes from daily searching in the Book of Mormon that can come in no other way. It not only gets us nearer to God and teaches us why we need Christ, but, as President Benson has said, there is something more:

> There is a power in the book which will begin to flow into your lives the moment you begin a serious study of the book. You will find greater power to resist temptation. You will find the power to avoid deception. You will find the power to stay on the strait and narrow path. The scriptures are called "the words of life" (see D&C 84:85), and nowhere is that more true than it is of the Book of Mormon. When you begin to hunger and thirst after those words, you will find life in greater and greater abundance. (*Ensign,* November 1986, p. 7.)

Why was President Benson so emphatic about using the Book of Mormon as it was intended to be used? Have we caught this vision as discussed in chapter 1? Do we feel what he felt? Do we see what he saw? Do we know what he knew? Why have he and all the other modern prophets so forcefully pleaded with the Saints to drink deeply from the glorious pages of the Book of Mormon? Perhaps a few quotes from some Apostles and prophets can help us answer the preceding question.

The Book of Mormon is the instrument that God designed to "sweep the earth as with a flood, to gather out [His] elect." (Moses 7:62.) This sacred volume of scripture needs to become more central in our preaching, our teaching, and our missionary work. . . .

The time is long overdue for a massive flooding of the earth with the Book of Mormon for the many reasons which the Lord has given. In this age of electronic media and mass distribution of the printed word, God will hold us accountable if we do not now move the Book of Mormon in a monumental way.

We have the Book of Mormon, we have the members, we have the missionaries, we have the resources, and the world has the need. The time is now!

My beloved brothers and sisters, we hardly fathom the power of the Book of Mormon, nor the divine role it must yet play, nor the extent to which it must be moved.

"Few men on the earth," said Elder Bruce R. McConkie, "either in or out of the Church, have caught the vision of what the Book of Mormon is all about. Few are they among men who know the part it has played and will yet play in preparing the way for the coming of Him of whom it is a new witness. . . . The Book of Mormon shall so affect men that the whole earth and all its peoples will have been influenced and governed by it. . . . There is no greater issue ever to confront mankind in modern times than this: Is the Book of Mormon the mind and will and voice of God to all men?" We testify that it is. (*Millennial Messiah*, pp. 159, 170, 179.) (Ezra Taft Benson, *Ensign*, November 1988, pp. 4–5.)

President Benson also suggested that because we have not been using the Book of Mormon as we should, our homes are not as strong as they could be, our families may be corrupted by worldly trends and teachings, our missionaries are not as effective, our Church classes are not as Spirit filled and our nation will continue to degenerate (see *Ensign,* November 1979, pp. 31–33).

He has further counseled: "Every Latter-day Saint should make the study of this book a lifetime pursuit. Otherwise he is placing his soul in jeopardy and neglecting that which could give spiritual and intellectual unity to his whole life. There is a difference between a convert who is built on the rock of Christ through the Book of Mormon and stays hold of that iron rod, and one who is not." (*Ensign,* May 1975, p. 65.)

These statements leave us asking some serious questions as to whether we are using the Book of Mormon as it was intended to be used. As mentioned in chapter 1, each of us must resolve really only two questions in our lives when it comes to religion. It matters not if we are members or nonmembers of The Church of Jesus Christ of Latter-day Saints. Is there a God? Is the Book of Mormon true? Upon those two questions hangs the balance of religious truth. Elder Bruce R. McConkie said it this way:

> These are deep and solemn and ponderous matters. We need not think we can trifle with sacred things and escape the wrath of a just God.
>
> Either the Book of Mormon is true, or it is false; either it came from God, or it was spawned in the infernal realms. It declares plainly that all men must accept it as pure scripture or they will lose their souls. It is not and cannot be simply another treatise on religion; it either came from heaven or from hell. And it is time for all those

who seek salvation to find out for themselves whether it is of the Lord or of Lucifer." (*Ensign,* November 1983, p. 73.)

We must find out for ourselves! In order to do that, we must read it with a sincere heart, ponder its pages, and ask the Lord if it is true (see Moroni 10:4–5). He will let us know. I am convinced that he wants us to know the truth. He knows that life eternal is to know the true nature of God and his Son whom he has sent (see John 3:16).

As President Benson has suggested, "We must flood the earth with the Book of Mormon and get out from under God's condemnation for having treated it lightly" (see *Ensign,* November 1988, p. 5.)

What is this condemnation that the entire Church is under? Why did the Lord use such powerful language as the Brethren returned from their missions in 1832? He said:

> And your minds in times past have been darkened because of unbelief, and because you have treated lightly the things you have received—
>
> Which vanity and unbelief have brought the whole church under condemnation.
>
> And this condemnation resteth upon the children of Zion, even all.
>
> And they shall remain under this condemnation until they repent and remember the new covenant, even the Book of Mormon and the former commandments which I have given them, not only to say, but to do according to that which I have written." (D&C 84:54–57.)

Certainly we must do better in sharing the Book of Mormon with the world. Certainly part of the condemnation is that our families are not as strong as they could be. But is this all that the condemnation consists of? I think not. Robert Millet, dean of the College of Religious Instruction at Brigham Young University, said this of the condemnation we are under:

> In a broader sense, I believe that the condemnation which rests upon the Latter-day Saints is a loss of spiritual power, a loss of blessings, a loss of perspective about eternal possibilities. Perhaps we have not enjoyed the revelation, the divine direction, the sweet promptings of the Spirit which could have been ours. We have not been the recipients of the fruit of the Spirit—"love, joy, peace, longsuffering, gentleness, goodness, faith, meekness, temperance" (Galatians 5:22–23) —like we could have been. Surely we have not enjoyed the understanding, the light and truth, the lens of pure intelligence which is so readily accessible. In too many cases, our minds and hearts have not been shaped and prepared by the Book of Mormon, by its lessons and logic, testimony and transforming power, and thus too often our judgment and discernment so essential to perceiving the false doctrines of the world, and even the irrelevant, has not been as strong as they might have been. Because we have not immersed and washed ourselves in those living waters which flow from the Book of Mormon, we have not enjoyed faith like the ancients, that faith which strengthens resolve and provides courage and peace in a time of unrest. So much of the stress and fear and apprehension and exhaustion that now exist in society is so very unnecessary; ours could be the right to that lifting and liberating Spirit which produces hope and peace and rest. Though the light of the fullness of the everlasting gospel has begun to break forth into a world of darkness (D&C 45:28), yet too often we walk in darkness at noonday, or at least we traverse the path of life in twilight when we might bask in the bright light of the Son. ("Lifting the Condemnation: The Sanctifying Power of the Book of Mormon," address presented at the Know the Book of Mormon seminar, Brigham Young University, 2 June 1990, p. 3.)

The Book of Mormon, this glorious treasure, has changed my life forever. I read it in Seminary in the ninth grade. However, I did so only to fulfill my assignment and didn't give it much thought. At age eighteen, I left home to enter the world of college football. At the time I hadn't decided whether I would serve a mission. I wanted to play football. I thought of little else.

One night after a home game, I went with some of my teammates to an activity in a nearby city. We arrived home about 8:30 A.M. the following morning. It was Sunday, and priesthood meeting started at 9:00 A.M. I showered and walked to church at the institute of religion across the street from our dormitory. As I walked in, the bishop greeted me. He asked me a few questions, and then we went to his office to talk. I don't remember all we talked about, but I remember going back to the dorm determined to read the Book of Mormon, pray, and find out if it were true!

When I arrived back at the dorm, I pulled my scriptures from the shelf. The scriptures were a high school graduation gift from my parents. The previous year in seminary I had not missed a day of reading the Doctrine and Covenants, but I had not read for the entire summer.

I opened the Book of Mormon and began reading. Before long some of my teammates walked in and began giving me a difficult time. After that, I decided to read in private. Every morning I got up early and read and prayed. To this day I can remember finishing Moroni 10 and applying the magnificent promise found in verses 4 and 5.

That day I discovered that the book is true and I needed to share it with others. Doing so, however, was not easy. I was on scholarship and was committed to play football. I felt my decision had been made. I would stay and play football and be a missionary by my actions.

Thanksgiving vacation came, and I returned home. After talking with my family, I went to visit my good friend Taylor Manning. Again, I thought my decision was made; that is, until I walked into Taylor's kitchen and saw him with a missionary haircut sitting at the table eating a bowl of cereal. "What happened to you?" I asked.

He responded, "I'm going on a mission, Ed!" (He always called me Ed for some reason.) He told me that he knew the Book of Mormon to be true and he wanted to serve his Father in Heaven. I knew it was true too . . . but, give up a football scholarship? I was stunned. However, it didn't take long before my testimony of the book, and Taylor's testimony, won the battle. When I went back to school, I talked with my coach and we worked out arrangements for when I would get back in two years. I went to the New Mexico and Arizona mission. Taylor went to the Netherlands. Neither of us would be where we are today had we not read and prayed about the Book of Mormon.

After coming home, I was able to play football for three more seasons. However, these last three seasons were focused on far more than just how far or how accurately I could throw a football. I had found out, to some extent, why I needed Christ.

We all need to learn why we need Christ, to become more like little children, and to feel the power of the word. By doing so, we can bring our lives under the infinite reaches of the Atonement and become not only *alive* in Christ but also *consumed* in Christ. This can happen if we will use the Book of Mormon properly and help lift the condemnation. We can't read the book like a fictional novel. We must use consistency and intensity to uncover some of its rich, rich treasures. As Elder Neal A. Maxwell has said:

Thus the Book of Mormon will be with us "as long as the earth shall stand." We need all that time to explore it, for the book is like a vast mansion with gardens, towers, courtyards, and wings. There are rooms yet to be entered, with flaming fireplaces waiting to warm us. The rooms glimpsed so far contain further furnishings and rich detail yet to be savored, but decor dating from Eden is evident. There are panels inlaid with incredible insights, particularly insights about the great question. Yet we as Church members sometimes behave like hurried tourists, scarcely venturing beyond the entry hall." (*Not My Will, but Thine* [Salt Lake City: Bookcraft, 1988], p. 33.)

8

"Beyond the Entry Hall"

In this chapter let us go "beyond the entry hall" (see Neal A. Maxwell, "*Not My Will, but Thine*," [Salt Lake City: Bookcraft, 1988], p. 33). Let us discuss and discover together some of the gardens, towers, courtyards, and wings. Perhaps we can be warmed by some of the flaming fireplaces that have been, for so long, waiting to warm us. In doing so, I would like to discuss more about lifting the condemnation that we as Church members are under and then accept the challenge issued by President Ezra Taft Benson to Church writers, teachers, and leaders. He said:

> I challenge our Church writers, teachers, and leaders to tell us more Book of Mormon conversion stories that will strengthen our faith and prepare great missionaries. Show us how to effectively use it as a missionary tool, and let us know how it leads us to Christ and answers our personal problems and those of the world.

I challenge those who are in business and other professions to see that there are copies of the Book of Mormon in their reception rooms.

I challenge owners of cassette players to play Book of Mormon cassettes from time to time and to listen to them at home and while walking, jogging, or driving.

I challenge the homes of Israel to display on their walls great quotations and scenes from the Book of Mormon.

I challenge all of us to prayerfully consider steps that we can personally take to bring this new witness for Christ more fully into our own lives and into a world that so desperately needs it. (*Ensign*, November 1988, pp. 5–6.)

This challenge is great and exciting! Could the condemnation be lifted if every Latter-day Saint accepted the challenge and let the people of the earth know about the powers of this glorious Book of Mormon? In addition to what we discussed in the previous chapter, what is this condemnation? Could part of it be that we don't have all the scriptures that the Lord would like to bless us with? Could all of the difficult questions that trouble so many people be answered if we had the sealed portion of the Book of Mormon, the records of the lost tribes of Israel, the record of the vision of the Brother of Jared, or the entirety of the teachings of Jesus? Remember that Mormon said that he did not even write "a hundredth part of the things which Jesus did truly teach unto the people" (3 Nephi 26:6).

Each year of teaching usually brings with it the same questions raised by inquiring students. They always want to know about the Creation, evolution, the second coming of Christ, and, of course, where did the dinosaurs come from if there was no death of any living creature before the Fall? I generally tell them that I'm not sure which of all the theories concerning the dinosaurs is true, but that I do know the dinosaurs were there and I know they're old because I've been to Vernal, Utah, and I've seen evidence of them! Then I tell them that the Book of Mormon has the answer to every one of these difficult questions. They always look surprised because most have read the book and don't remember anything about dinosaurs. We then discuss three sets of scripture verses that not only answer difficult questions but also help them better understand the condemnation we are under.

In 3 Nephi 26:3, the Savior, as a resurrected being while visiting the Americas, "did expound all things, even from the beginning until the time that he should come in his glory—yea, even all things which should come upon the face of the earth, even until the elements should melt with fervent heat, and the earth should be wrapt together as a scroll, and the heavens and the earth should pass away."

The Nephites and Lamanites of 34 A.D. knew everything about the Creation! They knew everything from the beginning to the end of the earth. Then Mormon commented:

> But behold the plates of Nephi do contain the more part of the things which he taught the people.
>
> And these things have I written, which are a lesser part of the things which he taught the people; and I have written them to the intent that they may be brought again unto this people, from the Gentiles, according to the words which Jesus hath spoken.
>
> And when they shall have received this, which is expedient that they should have first, to try their faith, and if it shall so be that they shall believe these things then shall the greater things be made manifest unto them.
>
> And if it so be that they will not believe these things, then shall the greater things be withheld from them, unto their condemnation. (3 Nephi 26:7–10.)

As I understand these passages, "these things" mean the Book of Mormon. If we do not utilize the portions of the Book of Mormon that we now possess, it will be "unto our condemnation"!

Mormon desired to make known unto us "all [that was] engraven upon the plates of Nephi, but the Lord forbade it, saying: I will try the faith of my people" (3 Nephi 26:11). Mormon knew! And he made it clear that we would not receive the remainder of Christ's teachings until we appropriately used that which we already have—mainly the Book of Mormon. Perhaps that is why the prophets continually ask us to read and reread the book and to flood the earth with it!

After reading and discussing these passages, we then read 2 Nephi 27:6–8, 10:

> And it shall come to pass that the Lord God shall bring forth unto you the words of a book, and they shall be the words of them which have slumbered.
>
> And behold the book shall be sealed; and in the book shall be a revelation from God, from the beginning of the world to the ending thereof.
>
> Wherefore, because of the things which are sealed up, the things which are sealed shall not be delivered in the day of the wickedness and abominations of the people. Wherefore the book shall be kept from them. . . .
>
> But the words which are sealed he shall not deliver, neither shall he deliver the book. For the book shall be sealed by the power of God, and the revelation which was sealed shall be kept in the book until the own due time of the Lord, that they may come forth; for behold, they reveal all things from the foundation of the world unto the end thereof.

Evidently, the sealed portion of the Book of Mormon contains a history of "all things from the foundation of the world unto the end thereof." Again, all the questions can be answered if we can lift the condemnation and receive all that the Lord desires us to have.

Of the return of these records, Elder Neal A. Maxwell wrote, "Today we carry convenient quadruple combinations of the scriptures, but one day, since more scriptures are coming, we may need to pull little red wagons brimful with books" (*A Wonderful Flood of Light* [Salt Lake City: Bookcraft, 1990], p. 18).

How exciting! With the advent of CD Rom and laptop computers, perhaps we won't need the wagons after all—just one or two CDs and a computer and all the records will be instantly brought up on a screen before our very eyes!

When discussing these passages with students, when time allows I love to take them to one other passage of scripture in the Book of Mormon, Ether 3:25–26 and 4:7:

> And when the Lord had said these words, he showed unto the brother of Jared all the inhabitants of the earth which had been, and also all that would be; and he withheld them not from his sight, even unto the ends of the earth.
>
> For he had said unto him in times before, that if he would believe in him that he could show unto him all things—it should be shown unto him; therefore the Lord could not withhold anything from him, for he knew that the Lord could show him all things. . . .
>
> And in that day that they shall exercise faith in me, saith the Lord, even as the brother of Jared did, that they may become sanctified in me, then will I manifest unto them the things which the brother of Jared saw, even to the unfolding unto them all my revelations, saith Jesus Christ, the Son of God, the Father of the heavens and of the earth, and all things that in them are.

We must use the Book of Mormon as the Lord intended so we can receive these other records. Then certainly the condemnation would begin to be lifted, and we could begin to know all things.

In the fall of 1976, something happened in my life that has become more sacred with each passing year. As I continue to learn more about our Father, his Son, and their gospel, the memory of these events becomes more humbling.

The first year I played football at Weber State in Ogden, Utah, I was the only returned missionary on the team. It was not easy at times, but it was exciting and rewarding.

One weekend we flew to St. Louis, Missouri, and then took a bus to Macomb, Illinois, where we were to play a game against Western Illinois University. The game was played on Saturday evening, so we had much of the day to prepare ourselves. After our Saturday morning meeting, I returned to the hotel and began to prepare for the game.

A knock came at the door. It was Ralph Hunter, one of our coaches. Coach Hunter and his dear wife, Shirley, were like parents to my wife and me. They were active members of the Church and understood some of my feelings about being the only returned missionary on a major college football team.

He stood at the door with a brown paper bag in his hand. He indicated that he wanted me to go with him for a couple of hours. I was somewhat hesitant because of the chiding of my roommates. They knew Coach Hunter was a Latter-day Saint, and they would tease me about being his pet and always getting favors from him.

He said that he wanted me to go because I would understand what I would see—I was married and had served a mission. I had no idea where we were going or what was in the paper bag; I just knew I should go, no matter what harassment I had to take from my teammates. That one decision forever influenced me. It was one of those milestone experiences that doesn't necessarily change a person but becomes an anchor, a reference point, that allows the individual in times of doubt or discouragement to cast his mind back upon the time when God so willingly spoke peace to his mind and gave him a witness (see D&C 6:23–24).

We walked through the rolling hills of Macomb and made our way through an old cemetery. As we journeyed, Coach Hunter told me that we were taking the Book of Mormon on cassette tape to a twenty-three-year-old man whom Coach Hunter's son had taught and baptized. His son had served as a missionary in Macomb some months prior to our visit. The paper bag contained the cassettes. He didn't share much more about the young man or his conversion because he said I would better understand once I met him.

As we approached the young man's home, we saw an older gentleman sitting in a rocking chair inside a screened porch, smoking a cigarette. He saw us on his walkway and arose to greet us. When he recognized Coach Hunter, he crushed the cigarette under his foot and extended his arms to hug him. Tears trickled down his cheeks as the two men hugged and exchanged warm greetings. I was introduced as a returned missionary football player.

The man called for his wife to come and see who was at the door. When she arrived, she was not nearly so warm and friendly to Coach Hunter as was her husband. When I was introduced as a former missionary, she looked at me and grunted, "Huh, huh, huh," and walked away. I remember wondering what on earth I had done to receive such a cold reception. The husband said not to be offended and then said, "Brian would love to meet you."

Who is Brian? I silently wondered. Then we entered the home. The smell of cleaning solution and antiseptic filled my nostrils. Everything in the room was meticulously clean. Then my eyes beheld Brian Foster for the first time.

To describe what Brian looked like is difficult. I was shocked. It hadn't occurred to me that he was as disabled as he was. I'm writing this story nearly twenty years after it occurred, so I will describe what he looked like and what happened after our introduction as best as I can remember.

He was lying on a covering of sheepskin to prevent bed sores. He was approximately three feet long and weighed at most sixty or seventy pounds. His arms and legs were terribly disfigured, and his skin was stretched tightly over his bones like a tight-fitting rubber glove on a hand. There was no muscle tissue that I could detect, just rough, leathery skin stretched over his completely disfigured body. His abdomen looked much like an oversized football or rugby ball, and his head was narrow, like two dinner plates face down on one another. His skin was pulled tightly on his face, which caused his teeth to stick almost straight out, and his eyes were sunken deep into dark sockets. To my knowledge he could not move any part of his body on his own other than his mouth and eyes.

He could read and talk with a low gruff voice. A large-letter edition of *Reader's Digest* and the Bible were sitting on a music stand next to his bed. His dad had to turn the pages for him, and reading tired him easily. That was the major reason that Coach Hunter wanted to bring the Book of Mormon on cassette tape. Then, instead of laboring to read the scriptures or having someone read them to him, Brian could just listen.

After the introduction, Brian looked at me and said,

"Pretty sad, huh?" I didn't know exactly what he was referring to, but then he put me at ease by saying something funny.

At that time, Coach Hunter explained that we were there to play a game that night and that his son had asked him to bring a special gift for Brian. Brian asked what it was, and Coach Hunter pulled the tapes from the paper bag. What happened next was incredible. Coach Hunter handed Brian the tapes and then said a few words on behalf of his son. Brian said nothing. He couldn't talk. I noticed a small pool of tears gather above the bridge of his nose and then burst over. As the tears dripped from his nose to his pillow, it was all I could do to keep my composure. After several minutes of teary silence, Brian said the only thing he could muster. Through tears in a quiet, raspy whisper, he said, "Thank you. Thank you. Thank you. Now I can be a missionary! Thank you."

After composing himself somewhat, he said, "I'll play these tapes every day, all day, on full blast! Anyone who comes to our home will hear the message of the Book of Mormon!"

All Brian could think about was sharing the truth of the Book of Mormon message and being a missionary. I almost shrunk in shame as I experienced being in the presence of this near-perfect young man.

For the next two hours or so, Brian and his dad shared with us his story of finding and converting to the Church. His mother never entered the room or said a word to us. From what Coach Hunter had told me, she was very bitter and angry with God for sending her a freak for a son.

Brian told us that after his birth he had needed constant attention. His dad stayed with him full time while his mother worked to support the three of them. Brian also suffered from an immune system deficiency so he was not allowed to leave his room, nor was he allowed visitors often, especially if they had been ill with anything. I then understood why everything smelled and looked so meticulously clean. Even our being there was a risk. However, he was willing to take it.

He continued with the story of how he and his dad had become so fed up with the various preachers and ministers not being able to answer his difficult questions about life that they concluded the answers were not found in organized religion.

Shortly after that decision was when my coach's son and his companion approached their home and knocked on the door. The Elders were turned away and told never to come back. However, a couple of months later, they came back anyway. They checked their tracting record for details of what had happened. They read the "don't come back" message but felt that they should try again. They were scared but felt inspired. When they knocked on the door, Mr. Foster answered. He went through the same routine and again told them not to return. The two dejected missionaries walked away wondering why they had felt inspired to knock on the door.

After they left, Brian inquired who was at the door and his dad responded, "Those blankety blank Mormons again!"

Brian told him they had never heard the Mormons and asked his dad to go get them and invite them in. Reluctantly, Mr. Foster returned to the door, opened it, and yelled for the missionaries to return.

The Elders were understandably hesitant to come back. Mr. Foster assured them it was okay. He and his son just wanted to hear their message.

When they entered the room and sat down, Brian asked them the same questions he had asked all the others: "Why did God make me this way? How come my mother will have nothing to do with me and thinks I'm a freak of nature?"

I don't remember how Brian said the Elders answered, but he said that when they shared the plan of salvation and the Joseph Smith story and bore simple, humble testimonies of Christ, he knew it was true.

It took several weeks to teach Brian because they could only come once a week. However, the day arrived when he was ready to be baptized. The only problem was that Brian, because of his illness, had not been outside in twenty-three years. He asked the Elders if he could be baptized in his bathtub. They called the mission president and were told to find another way.

When they told Brian, they were discouraged and very frustrated. Then Brian became the teacher rather than the student. He stunned the Elders with his bold question.

"Elders, don't you have any faith? You've been teaching me about faith all these weeks and you don't have any! Don't you believe that we can pray and fast for a perfect day so I can go outside without getting sick and be baptized into the Lord's true church?"

How would you have answered such a direct, bold question? The Elders didn't know what to say. So they set a date for the baptism and, following Brian's orders, they all prayed and fasted for a perfect day.

The day arrived, and the Elders wrapped Brian in blankets, placed him lying down in the backseat of the car, and headed for the baptism.

Brian then told me how wonderful it was to look up through the window and see limbs of trees passing by. He said it was magnificent to hear all the sounds that he had only heard previously from a television.

Never in his life had he experienced all the common things that you and I take for granted every day. He had never run on the grass with bare feet. Never thrown a snowball or been to a movie, a dance, or a ball game. He had never seen nor smelled the ocean or the mountains. This day in the car was like being "born again."

He told me one of his favorite things was seeing telephone lines stretched from pole to pole. He said, "I always wondered how a phone worked." We laughed many times as he told his story.

He continued with how he felt when the Elders wrapped him in a white sheet because no clothes would fit his disfigured body. Four Elders went into the water with him, and one offered the baptismal prayer. Then all four lowered him into the water. After coming up out of the water, the missionaries quickly took the wet sheet from off his body, wrapped him up again in blankets, and rushed him home to confirm him and ordain him to the Aaronic Priesthood.

As he finished telling me the story, he said, "So, here I am. And now you guys have given me an opportunity to be a missionary. Thank you, thank you, thank you."

As this story is being written, even now, nearly twenty years later, my heart swells with emotion as I ponder what happened just before Coach Hunter and I had to leave to prepare for our ball game that night.

Brian quietly asked me to place my hand on his shoulder so he could feel my touch as he bore his testimony. I did so with some apprehension. He rolled his eyes in my direction, looked me squarely in the eye, and said, "You and I will probably never see each other again in this life. However, hopefully we will up there," motioning with his eyes upward. I then made some comment about teaching him how to play ball in the next life, when his body was whole. His eyes then filled up with tears. "Thanks, my friend, for allowing me to be a missionary and share the Book of Mormon."

I left Brian's home a new man. I hardly remember anything about the game that night. All I could think about was Brian's testimony and his desire to be a missionary by sharing the Book of Mormon with anyone who came into earshot of the sound of his tape recorder.

Time passed quickly and that season of football ended. School was difficult and I was so busy that I didn't think a great deal about Brian. Then one day I received a message to meet with Coach Hunter in his office. I had no idea what he wanted, so my mind did crazy things as I walked toward the stadium. I wondered if I was going to lose my scholarship for some reason. It didn't help when I walked in and Coach Hunter was very serious. After asking me to sit down, he looked at me and tears filled his eyes.

"Jack," he said, "I received a call from Brian's dad yesterday and thought you would like to know that Brian passed away yesterday. You should also know that the Book of Mormon was playing on his recorder when he died."

I cried hard that day. Brian had been right. We never would see each other or talk again in this life. Our ball game would have to be in another life. But it would sure be fun to play basketball with Brian having a perfect body. I realized that day in Coach Hunter's office how much I loved and admired Brian.

As the school year was coming to a close, Coach Hunter asked me to speak in his sacrament meeting before I left for the summer. Just before the meeting, Coach Hunter told me that he had received a call from Brian's mother that afternoon, and Brian's mom and dad had been baptized the day before. Words cannot describe the excitement that rushed through me as he told me what had happened.

Day after day, Brian's mother kept hearing the powerful messages of the Book of Mormon as Brian played the tapes. When Brian died, his mother finally realized what she had done to her son by barely acknowledging him. The pain of never having held him in her arms and never having told him that she loved him was haunting. I couldn't believe that Coach was talking about the same lady who had simply said, "Huh, huh, huh," and walked away.

He said that she had been feeling so bad that she called the mission president and told him her story. She told him she felt something she couldn't describe when she heard the words of the Book of Mormon. She wanted to know if she could be forgiven and if there were any possibility of her ever seeing or being with her son again. She wanted to make it up to him.

I'll bet the mission president nearly fell out of his chair! He sent his two assistants to teach Mrs. Foster, and she gained a testimony and desired baptism. Her husband was now the one who balked at the idea. He felt that Brian's death was the fault of the missionaries because they took him outside to baptize him. Mrs. Foster simply said, "I'm going to be with our son again, with or without you!" Her mighty change must have stirred him a little because he was baptized with her.

I have no idea what has happened to the Fosters since then, but I know that Brian received his wish—he was a missionary! His only two direct converts were his parents. Maybe his story can touch some of the readers of this book enough to want to join the Church, get reactivated, stay strong in the Church, or most of all, get into the glorious Book of Mormon! This book can and will change lives!

Perhaps Brian's story can help us use the Book of Mormon properly so we can begin to get out from under the condemnation that the entire Church is under by remembering the new covenant, even the Book of Mormon (see D&C 84:54–57).

Hopefully his story will also help us all appreciate what we have in our lives and inspire us to use it to bless the lives of others. Hopefully Brian's example of bravery and faith will help us all want to be brave sons and brave daughters of Almighty God. May we be brave enough to pursue our dreams and our freedom! It will be difficult, but we can do it. I know we can!

The words of Elder Neal A. Maxwell put this entire chapter into perspective. He said, "The special spirits who have been reserved to live in this time of challenges and who overcome, will one day be praised for their stamina by those who pulled handcarts" (*Notwithstanding My Weakness* [Salt Lake City: Deseret Book Co., 1981], p. 18).

Someday, God willing, and I believe he is, we will not only greet "those who pulled handcarts," but we will hopefully meet Brian Foster. We will fall upon their necks, and they upon ours, and we will rejoice together. And maybe, just maybe, we will even be able to shoot a few baskets or throw a football or two together!

9

This Life Is the Time to Prepare

Many topics have been discussed in this book. All of them—from dreaming dreams to freedom of religion, from being brave to withstanding sexual pressure, from following the simple formula of having the Spirit to the correct use of the Book of Mormon—have been built upon one another. We need them all. We need to put them together in such a way that allows us to synergize our approach to living life to the fullest and stay close to our Father and his Son in the process. By doing so we learn to live in the world but not be of the world. President Marion G. Romney taught:

> It has been my experience that you have to seek the Lord until you get out of the influence of this world, because this world is so much controlled by the things that are not of the Lord.
>
> On occasions in my life, I have wanted to get in touch

with the Lord, and I have wanted to get in touch with him bad enough that I have fasted at regular intervals over long periods of time. I testify to you that God is available on those terms.

If you pray frequently, live the gospel and abide by its principles, you will be all right. You will be successful in your chosen professions and above all you will succeed in life. I know these things are true. I am not talking to you about fables; I am talking to you about the facts of eternal life. I have tried them all and I know they are true." (Brigham Young University Fireside, 16 October 1966; also cited in F. Burton Howard, *Marion G. Romney: His Life and Faith* [Salt Lake City: Bookcraft, 1988], p. 225.)

When we prepare for life in this manner, we will not fail, and we will never need to fear! This life is a time to prepare! We need not make serious mistakes in our lives if we can somehow learn to walk by the Spirit. On this subject, President Romney again taught a powerful lesson of paying the price to prepare to receive the Spirit's guidance and direction:

I know from my own experience that prayer is the pathway by which we may come into contact with God and receive direction from him. There have been times in my life when it was very difficult for me to get through to the Lord and when I've had to fast and pray for periods each week over long months of time. But it can be done, and you can pray to the Father and receive help in your problems. One need not make serious mistakes in life. If you can learn to walk by the Spirit, you can make every decision in your life correctly. ("Spiritual Communication," *Improvement Era*, April 1966, p. 275; also cited in *Marion G. Romney: His Life and Faith*, p. 227.)

"There are some people in the world today . . . who know that God is their Father and that he is not far from them. If they were to speak on the subject, they would tell you that of all their possessions, this knowledge is the most precious. From it they obtain power to resist temptation, courage in times of danger, companionship in hours of loneliness, and comfort in sorrow. This knowledge of God gives them faith and hope that tomorrow will be better than today. It is an anchor to their soul which gives purpose to life, although all men and things about them be in confusion and chaos. They know that such conditions have come because men are without that knowledge and are therefore not guided by God." (As cited in F. Burton Howard, *Marion G. Romney: His Life and Faith,* pp. 227–28.)

Is this one of the lessons Isaiah was trying to teach in his wonderful discourse on fasting? He taught that when we pay the price to fast and pray properly, "then shall thy light break forth as the morning, and thine health shall spring forth speedily: and thy righteousness shall go before thee; the glory of the Lord shall be thy rereward. Then shalt thou call, and the Lord shall answer; thou shalt cry, and he shall say, Here I am." (Isaiah 58:8–9.)

The Savior gave a similar answer to the early Saints as the mob persecution in Missouri intensified in August 1833:

> Verily I say unto you my friends, fear not, let your hearts be comforted; yea, rejoice evermore, and in everything give thanks;
>
> Waiting patiently on the Lord, for your prayers have entered into the ears of the Lord of Sabaoth, and are recorded with this seal and testament—the Lord hath sworn and decreed that they shall be granted.
>
> Therefore, he giveth this promise unto you, with an immutable covenant that they shall be fulfilled; and all things wherewith you have been afflicted shall work together for your good, and to my name's glory, saith the Lord. (D&C 98:1–3.)

The Lord does hear us! He does help us, but always in his own way and when it is expedient. But we must prepare. Is this not what Amulek was trying to teach? He taught, "This life is the time for men to prepare to meet God; yea, behold the day of this life is the day for men to perform their labors" (Alma 34:32).

This entire concept of paying the price to prepare now and to live life to the fullest, yet always striving to walk in the Spirit, was seered into my heart by an experience with one of my childhood friends.

As boys, Jeff and Gary Geertsen and I were inseparable. We walked to school together, played almost every sport imaginable together, ate together, and slept at each others' homes. We built underground huts together, rode horses together, and, with the help of their dad, we even built an eighteen-hole putting golf course around their yard. It was a wonderful life together.

Our friendship endured many troubled times. My dog killed a litter of their kittens, but our friendship survived. Their younger sister accidently knocked my younger sister's teeth out by hitting her in the mouth with a golf club. But our friendship stayed intact. In fact, we looked for my sister Becky's teeth together on the Geertsen's front lawn. Again, it was wonderful.

Then that awful day arrived when the Geertsens moved, and we ended up going to different high schools. However, time and distance did not dim our love for one another.

The years passed. We each grew up, served missions, and went on with our lives. One day a few years ago, Jeff and Gary's sister Kristine called me on the phone to ask me to go to the hospital. She said Gary was in the advanced stages of leukemia and might not make it much longer.

I was troubled that I hadn't been contacted sooner.

Kristine told me the reason for not calling sooner was that she and Gary were going to Seattle for a bone marrow transplant and felt that he was going to be okay. However, Gary had taken a turn for the worse, and she wanted to make sure I saw him before they left for Seattle.

The lessons Gary taught me that day have been a great strength. They have motivated me on many occasions to take advantage of the life I have right now, today! As we visited, he in his swollen, bald condition and I in my hospital gown and mask, I rubbed his swollen feet. Tears streamed down my face into the mask as we reminisced about our glorious childhood. He then asked when I was to speak next. I informed him, and he proceeded to tell me what he had learned; then he asked me to take some notes so that I could tell some of the people I would speak to what he had to say. I wrote all the notes on a five-by-seven card that has become priceless to me. (I gave the original to his wife after his death, but I keep a photocopy of it with me in my speaking notes.)

The words he shared were simple. Yet, coming from a man who felt he would be standing before his Maker at any moment gave them deep meaning. He said: "When someone pulls out the stopwatch you begin to look at things a whole lot different. When they stop the clock it's simply different." He talked of Alma chapter 34. He stressed that "this life is the time for men to prepare to meet [their] God."

He then talked of the importance of Alma 37:35 and getting the young people to "learn in [their] youth to keep the commandments of God."

He talked of how he felt when he woke up one morning and couldn't see out of one eye. He went to the doctor, then later found out he was in the advanced stages of leukemia and had less than thirty days to live. At the time we talked, he had made it through seven weeks and hoped that the bone marrow transplant would extend his life even longer.

He asked me to emphasize 2 Nephi 28:7–8 and to plead with people not to "eat, drink, and be merry," but to take time to appreciate every minute of their lives.

As we talked, I continued to rub his swollen feet and to cry. I tried to tell him he wasn't going to die, but he told me to get real and accept the fact that his time on earth was over. He then told me of a walk he had gone on the day before with his parents, wife, and daughter. His father pushed him in a wheelchair as they walked, talked, and cried some. He said he didn't want to go back inside the hospital. He just wanted to view "Y" mountain and watch the softball game being played by some Provo High School P.E. students. He wanted to take it all in and "have one more good look," because these sights would be his last memories of earth. He said he hoped he could leave the hospital for three or four hours the following day so he could have one last family portrait and then attend one last session at the temple with his wife.

He then taught me two profound truths. He said: "Jack, tell people that I've learned we can endure an awful lot of pain in this life and to never, never give up on life."

Our conversation came to a close with one last lesson. "Tell people from me," he said, "that what really matters in this life is God, family, friends, and home." I left the hospital that Tuesday afternoon a different man. I never saw Gary alive again. The bone marrow transplant didn't take, and he died a couple of weeks later. However, his memory and the memory of him and Jeff and me and our boyhood goes on. Jeff and I still see each other often, and our love as friends is deeper now than ever.

God, family, friends, and home. To a dying man, these are what mattered. Is this not what the restoration of the gospel of Jesus Christ is all about? Is it not to know and love the only true and living God? Is it not to have our families sealed to us for time and all eternity? Is it not to love our friends and neighbors as ourselves and to have happy and productive homes? Is it not to return home to the temple and to that God who gave us life? Cannot these four simple things be what all mankind dream dreams about and see visions of the future? Is this why men, women, and children who finally turn their lives over to God find out one of the "hidden treasures of knowledge": that God can do more with their lives than they can do with themselves? This is why we must be brave! This is why we must maintain our freedom of religion and immerse ourselves in the living waters of the Book of Mormon so we can, as Malachi prophesied, "turn the heart of the fathers to the children, and the heart of the children to their fathers, lest I come and smite the earth with a curse" (Malachi 4:6). With the work and glory (see Moses 1:39) of our Father at the center of our lives, we can do as President Ezra Taft Benson taught us all:

> "Men and women who turn their lives over to God will discover that He can make a lot more out of their lives than they can. He will deepen their joys, expand their vision, quicken their minds, strengthen their muscles, lift their spirits, multiply their blessings, increase their opportunities, comfort their souls, raise up friends, and pour out peace. Whosoever will lose his life in the service of God will find eternal life (see Matthew 10:39). (*The Teachings of Ezra Taft Benson* [Salt Lake City: Bookcraft, 1988], p. 361.)

Index